C. R Eliot, C. J Staples

A Manual for Use at Funerals

C. R Eliot, C. J Staples

A Manual for Use at Funerals

ISBN/EAN: 9783337371821

Printed in Europe, USA, Canada, Australia, Japan

Cover: Foto ©Lupo / pixelio.de

More available books at **www.hansebooks.com**

A

MANUAL

FOR USE AT

FUNERALS

CONSISTING OF

SCRIPTURE READINGS, POEMS, AND PROSE
SELECTIONS FROM VARIOUS SOURCES

BOSTON
PRINTED FOR THE COMPILERS
1886

CONTENTS.

	PAGE
SCRIPTURE SELECTIONS	1–79
A General Service	1
Prayers	7
Life	9
The Life of the Body	11
The Life of the Spirit	14
The Deep Waters	15
Sudden Death	18
Trial and Suffering	20
The Will of God	22
Aspiration	25
God our Comfort	27
God our Refuge	30
The Fruit of the Spirit	36
Uprightness and Fidelity	36
Wisdom and Worth	40
Patience	51
Gentleness and Love	53
Friendship	57
Purity and Humility	59
Joy and Faith	61
Children	63
Men and Women	66
The Aged	69
Life Immortal	71

CONTENTS.

THOUGHTS OF IMMORTALITY 80
SELECTED POEMS 107–210
    LIFE AND DEATH 107
    RESIGNATION — TRUST 133
    A GOOD LIFE 157
    SUFFERING AND REST 168
    CHILDHOOD AND YOUTH 183
    THE AGED 205
INDEX OF FIRST LINES 211
SUPPLEMENTARY LIST OF POEMS 215
ADDITIONAL PRAYERS 227

PREFACE.

THIS manual has been compiled in hope of assisting ministers and laymen in the task of preparing and conducting funeral services. Each occasion of bereavement is different from all others, and each funeral service requires special preparation. While, therefore, a "general service," containing selections appropriate to the majority of occasions, has been arranged, it is offered with the idea of being shortened and supplemented according to the judgment of the minister and the special circumstances that may arise. For this purpose we have brought together all passages of scripture which seemed appropriate, and have grouped them under various headings, so that anyone, with comparatively little trouble, can form the special service he needs.

While the manual is compiled with reference to its use at funerals, it is hoped that the selections here made, of prose and poetry, may be of service, also, as devotional readings, in the sick room or elsewhere.

The choice of poems was not an easy task. Many favorites will be missed, no doubt, and it cannot be hoped that the poems given will be of equal value to all. We have selected, as far as possible, those which have already proved their fitness for such uses.

With very few exceptions, the poems are given without change, since every clergyman will feel at liberty to make his own alterations, if they are deemed necessary. For lack of space, however, many of the poems have been shortened by the omission of stanzas irrelevant to funeral occasions. Such will be found marked with a star in the index of first lines. We have not printed hymns easily accessible in the Revised Hymn and Tune Book of the American Unitarian Association, though many of them are specially appropriate.

A supplementary list of poems which may be found serviceable with slight changes, has been added. Selections from extra-biblical scriptures, and from various writers, ancient and modern, have also been made, in the belief that they will be useful, if not as readings in the service itself, then as suggestive thoughts. A few prayers, original and selected, are given for the use of laymen called upon to conduct funeral services.

The compilers are indebted to the kindness of many friends for the suggestions they have made and the assistance they have given. Special acknowledgment is due to Messrs. Houghton, Mifflin & Co., Roberts Brothers, and others, for their courtesy in permitting the use of copyright poems.

CHRISTOPHER R. ELIOT.
CHARLES J. STAPLES.

SELECTIONS AND POEMS.

A GENERAL SERVICE.

LORD, thou hast been our dwelling-place in all generations. Before the mountains were brought forth, or ever thou hadst formed the earth and the world, even from everlasting to everlasting, thou art God. Thou turnest man to destruction; and sayest, Return, ye children of men. For a thousand years in thy sight are but as yesterday when it is past, and as a watch in the night. Thou carriest them away as with a flood; they are as a sleep: in the morning they are like grass which groweth up. In the morning it flourisheth, and groweth up; in the evening it is cut down, and withereth. The days of our years are three score years and ten; and if by reason of strength they be four score years, yet is their strength labor and sorrow; for it is soon cut off, and we fly away. So teach us to number our days, that we may apply our hearts unto wisdom. O satisfy us early with thy mercy; that we may rejoice and be glad all our days. Make us glad according to the days wherein thou hast afflicted us, and the years wherein we have seen evil. Let thy work appear unto thy servants, and thy glory unto their children. And let the beauty of the Lord our God be upon us: and establish thou the work of our hands upon us; yea, the work of our hands establish thou it.

Man that is born of a woman is of few days, and full of trouble. He cometh forth like a flower, and is cut down: he fleeth also as a shadow, and continueth not. Thou sendest forth thy spirit, they are created: and thou renewest the face of the earth. Thou hidest thy face, they are troubled: thou takest away their breath, they die, and return to their dust. For all men have one entrance into life, and the like going out. Ye know not what shall be on the morrow. For what is your life? It is even a vapour, that appeareth for a little time, and then vanisheth away. For we know in part, and we prophesy in part. But when that which is perfect is come, then that which is in part shall be done away. For now we see through a glass, darkly; but then face to face: now I know in part; but then shall I know even as also I am known.

O Lord, I know that the way of man is not in himself: it is not in man that walketh to direct his steps. The floods have lifted up, O Lord; the floods have lifted up their voice; the floods lift up their waves. Deep calleth unto deep at the noise of thy waterspouts: all thy waves and thy billows are gone over me. I am so troubled that I cannot speak. I call to remembrance my song in the night; I commune with mine own heart. Will the Lord cast off forever? and will he be favourable no more? Hath God forgotten to be gracious? And I said, This is my infirmity: but I will remember the years of the right hand of the Most High. Woe is me for my hurt! my wound is grievous: but I said, Truly this is a grief, and I must bear it. Not as I will, but as thou wilt: the spirit indeed is willing, but the flesh is weak; O my Father, if this cup may not pass away from me, except I drink it, thy will be done.

The Lord is my light and my salvation; whom shall I fear? The Lord is the strength of my life; of whom shall I be afraid? The Lord is good, a strong hold in the day of trouble; and he knoweth them that trust in him. Like as a father pitieth his children, so the Lord pitieth them that fear him. For he knoweth our frame, he remembereth that we are dust. Hast thou not known? hast thou not heard, that the everlasting God, the Lord, the creator of the ends of the earth, fainteth not, neither is weary? there is no searching of his understanding. He giveth power to the faint; and to them that have no might he increaseth strength. Even the youths shall faint and be weary, and the young men shall utterly fall. But they that wait upon the Lord shall renew their strength; they shall mount up with wings as eagles; they shall run, and not be weary; and they shall walk, and not faint Wait on the Lord: be of good courage and he shall strengthen thine heart: wait, I say, on the Lord.

The Lord is my shepherd; I shall not want. He maketh me to lie down in green pastures: he leadeth me beside the still waters. He restoreth my soul: he leadeth me in the paths of righteousness for his name's sake. Yea, though I walk through the valley of the shadow of death, I will fear no evil: for thou art with me: thy rod and thy staff they comfort me. Thou preparest a table before me in the presence of mine enemies: thou anointest my head with oil; my cup runneth over. Surely goodness and mercy shall follow me all the days of my life: and I will dwell in the house of the Lord for ever.

Jesus said unto her, I am the resurrection. and the life: he that believeth in me, though he were dead, yet shall he live; and whosoever liveth and believeth in me shall never die.   Let not your heart be troubled: ye believe in God, believe also in me. In my Father's house are many mansions: if it were not so, I would have told you. I go to prepare a place for you.   And if I go and prepare a place for you, I will come again, and receive you unto myself; that where I am, there ye may be also.

We brought nothing into this world, and it is certain that we can carry nothing out.   The Lord gave, and the Lord hath taken away; blessed be the name of the Lord.

But as touching the resurrection of the dead, have ye not read that which was spoken unto you by God, saying, I am the God of Abraham, and the God of Isaac, and the God of Jacob? God is not the God of the dead, but of the living.

But some man will say, How are the dead raised up? and with what body do they come? That which thou sowest is not quickened, except it die: and that which thou sowest, thou sowest not that body that shall be, but bare grain, it may chance of wheat, or of some other grain: but God giveth it a body as it has pleased him, and to every seed his own body.   There is one glory of the sun, and another glory of the moon, and another glory of the stars; for one star differeth from another star in glory. So also is the resurrection of the dead. It is sown in corruption, it is raised in incorruption; it is sown in dishonour, it is raised in glory: it is sown in weakness, it is raised in power: it is sown a natural body, it is raised a spiritual body. There is a natural body, and there is a spiritual body. As is the earthy, such are they also that are earthy: and as is the heavenly, such are they also that are heavenly. And as we have borne the image of the earthy, we shall also bear the image of the heavenly. Now this I say, brethren, that flesh and blood cannot inherit the kingdom of God; neither can corruption inherit incorruption. For this corruptible must put on incorruption, and this mortal must put on immortality. So when this corruptible shall have put on incorruption, and this mortal shall have put on immortality, then shall be brought to pass the saying that is written, Death is swallowed up in victory. O death, where is thy sting? O grave, where is thy victory? The sting of death is sin; and the strength of sin is the law. But thanks be to God, which giveth us the victory through our Lord Jesus Christ. Therefore, my beloved brethren, be ye steadfast, unmovable, always abounding in the work of the Lord, forasmuch as ye know that your labor is not in vain in the Lord.

I reckon that the sufferings of the present time are not worthy to be compared with the glory which shall be revealed to us. For eye hath not seen, nor ear heard, nor the heart of man conceived, the things which God hath prepared for them that love him. Our light affliction, which is but for a moment, worketh for us a far more exceeding and eternal weight of glory; while we look not at the things which are seen, but at the things which are not seen; for the things which are seen are temporal, but the things which are not seen are eternal. For we know that, if our earthly house of this tabernacle were dissolved, we have a building of God, a house not made with hands, eternal in the heavens. Whom the Lord loveth, he chasteneth. If ye endure chastening, God dealeth with you as with sons. Now no chastening for the present seemeth to be joyous, but grievous; nevertheless, afterward it yieldeth the peaceable fruit of righteousness unto them that are exercised thereby. The trying of your faith worketh patience. Submit yourselves to God, and the Lord will raise you up.

And I saw a new heaven and a new earth; for the first heaven and the first earth were passed away; and there was no more sea. And I heard a great voice out of heaven saying, Behold, the tabernacle of God is with men, and he will dwell with them, and they shall be his people, and God himself shall be with them, and be their God. And God shall wipe away all tears from their eyes; and there shall be no more death, neither sorrow, nor crying, neither shall there be any more pain: for the former things have passed away. And he that sat upon the throne said, Behold I make all things new. I am Alpha and Omega, the beginning and the end. I will give unto him that is athirst of the fountain of the water of life freely. He that overcometh shall inherit all things; and I will be his God, and he shall be my son. And I heard a voice from heaven saying unto me, Write. Blessed are the dead which die in the Lord from henceforth: yea, saith the Spirit, that they may rest from their labors; and their works do follow them. And, behold, I come quickly; and my reward is with me, to give every man according as his works shall be. I am Alpha and Omega, the beginning and the end, the first and the last. Blessed are they that do his commandments, that they may have right to the tree of life, and may enter in through the gates into the city.

I.

Almighty God, we come to thee because we need thee. Without thee we are poor and weak, and with thee we can be brave and strong. We bow ourselves before thy will. We yield ourselves to thy law. Thou sendest forth thy Spirit, we are created; thou takest away our breath, we die and return to the dust. In death as in life, in sorrow as in joy, thou art waiting to bless us, if we will but turn to thee. Thou dost gird and guide us, though we know it not; and the shadow with which thou darkenest our way is but the shadow of thy close-approaching and over-brooding presence.

Help us to find thee thus this day. Lead us from our weakness to thy strength, and from our ignorance to thy wisdom, and give to us the peace and confidence which walks in the darkness even as in the light. It is thou who dost take to thyself the life of this, thy servant. Help us to say and to believe that it is well, — well with the life which seems to go away, because it finds thy rest and peace, and well for us who stay, because of tender memories and Christian hopes. In the midst of grief and solitude give to us the prayer of gratitude and praise. As we perceive that the things which are seen are temporal, so much the more may we find that the things which are unseen are eternal. Strengthen in us that immortal hope which is ours in the discipleship of Jesus. Make us know that if our earthly house be dissolved, we have a building of God, a house not made with hands, eternal in the heavens; and, amid the sufferings of this present time, unveil to us the things which eye hath not seen, but which God hath prepared for them that love him.

Sanctify thus to these hearts the sorrow which thou

dost call upon them to bear. May they hear that voice which says, " Blessed are they that mourn, for they shall be comforted." As they walk through the valley of the shadow of death, may thy rod and staff support them, and may they be grateful for that Eternal Love which summons souls to rest from their labors, and dost permit them to enter into thy peace. Send us all back to our lives more eager to serve thee, and more inclined to love thee, as though in this mysterious presence we had learned to know the deeper meaning and responsibility of life. Amid the changes of this world make us strong and calm, because we rest in thee, and finally persuade us that neither death nor life, nor things present, nor things to come, shall be able to separate us from the love of God which is in Christ Jesus, our Lord. *Amen.*

F. G. P.

II.

O FATHER, we would not forget thy benefits. For life we thank thee; the throbbing life of Nature; the quick-beating pulse of human hearts, the swift flight of the spirit's prayer, the life eternal. For love we thank thee; that love which, from childhood onward, has been ours, blessing us, saving us, creating us anew. For hope we thank thee, and for light; for all that quickens faith; for the mind and heart of Christ; for the in-flowing of thy Spirit.

O God, we call thee, and thou art here. We are not strong; grant us thy strength. We cannot see; grant us thy light. We do not know the way; lead us, O Father, by thy Spirit. We falter, we wander, we dare not speak; only teach thou us to pray. So, in us, and through us, may thy kingdom come, and thy will be done. *Amen.*

C. R. E.

LIFE.

The ungodly said, reasoning with themselves, but not aright, Our life is short and tedious, and in the death of a man there is no remedy: neither was there any man known to have returned from the grave. For we are born at all adventure: and we shall be hereafter as though we had never been: for the breath in our nostrils is as smoke, and a little spark in the moving of our heart: which being extinguished, our body shall be turned into ashes, and our spirit shall vanish as the soft air, and our name shall be forgotten in time, and no man shall have our works in remembrance, and our life shall pass away as the trace of a cloud, and shall be dispersed as a mist, that is driven away with the beams of the sun, and overcome with the heat thereof. For our time is a very shadow that passeth away; and after our end there is no returning: for it is fast sealed, so that no man cometh again. Come on therefore, let us enjoy the good things that are present: and let us speedily use the creatures like as in youth. Let us fill ourselves with costly wine and ointments: and let no flower of the spring pass by us: let us crown ourselves with rosebuds, before they be withered: let none of us go without his part of our voluptuousness: let us leave tokens of our joyfulness in every place: for this is our portion, and our lot is this. Such things they did imagine, and were deceived: for their own wickedness hath blinded them. As for the mysteries of God, they knew them not: neither hoped they for the wages of righteousness, nor discerned a reward for blameless souls. For God created man to be immortal, and made him to be an image of his own eternity. [*Wisdom ii.*]

The souls of the righteous are in the hand of God, and there shall no torment touch them. In the sight of the unwise they seemed to die: and their departure is taken for misery, and their going from us to be utter destruction: but they are in peace. For though they be punished in the sight of men, yet is their hope full of immortality. And having been a little chastised, they shall be greatly rewarded: for God proved them, and found them worthy for himself. As gold in the furnace hath he tried them, and received them as a burnt offering. [*Wisdom iii.*]

To every thing there is a season, and a time to every purpose under the heaven: a time to be born, and a time to die; a time to plant, and a time to pluck up that which is planted; a time to kill, and a time to heal; a time to break down, and a time to build up; a time to weep, and a time to laugh; a time to mourn, and a time to dance; a time to rend, and a time to sew; a time to keep silence, and a time to speak; a time to love, and a time to hate; a time of war, and a time of peace. What profit hath he that worketh in that wherein he laboreth? I have seen the travail, which God hath given to the sons of men to be exercised in it. He hath made every thing beautiful in his time: also he hath set the world in their heart, so that no man can find out the work that God maketh from the beginning to the end. I know that there is no good in them, but for a man to rejoice, and to do good in his life. And also that every man enjoy the good of all his labor, it is the gift of God. I know that, whatsoever God doeth, it shall be forever: nothing can be put to it, nor any thing taken from it: and God doeth it, that men should fear before him. That which hath been is now; and that which is to be hath already been; and God requireth that which is past. [*Eccl. iii.*]

O death, how bitter is the remembrance of thee to a man that liveth at rest in his possessions, unto the man that hath nothing to vex him, and that hath prosperity in all things: yea, unto him that is yet able to receive meat! O death, acceptable is thy sentence unto the needy, and unto him whose strength faileth, that is now in the last age, and is vexed with all things, and to him that despaireth, and hath lost patience! Fear not the sentence of death, remember them that have been before thee, and that come after; for this is the sentence of the Lord over all flesh. [*Ecclus. xli.*]

None of us liveth to himself, and no man dieth to himself. For whether we live, we live unto the Lord; and whether we die, we die unto the Lord: whether we live therefore, or die, we are the Lord's. [*Rom. xiv.*]

THE LIFE OF THE BODY.

Man that is born of a woman is of few days, and full of trouble. He cometh forth like a flower, and is cut down: he fleeth also as a shadow, and continueth not. [*Job xiv.*] One dieth in his full strength, being wholly at ease and quiet. And another dieth in the bitterness of his soul, and never eateth with pleasure. They shall lie down alike in the dust, and the worms shall cover them. [*Job xxi.*] As the cloud is consumed and vanisheth away; so he that goeth down to the grave shall come up no more. He shall return no more to his house, neither shall his place know him any more. [*Job vii.*] For all men have one entrance into life, and the like going out. [*Wisdom vii.*] Here have we no continuing city, but we seek one to come. [*Heb. xiii.*] Now my days are swifter than a post: they are passed away as the swift ships: as the eagle that hasteth to the prey. [*Job ix.*] My days are swifter than a weaver's shuttle. [*Job vii.*] As the Lord liveth, and as thy soul liveth, there is but a step between me and death. [*1 Sam. xx.*]

If he set his heart upon man, if he gather unto himself his spirit and his breath; all flesh shall perish together, and man shall turn again unto dust. In a moment shall they die, and the people shall be troubled at midnight, and pass away: and the mighty shall be taken away without hand. For his eyes are upon the ways of man, and he seeth all his goings. There is no darkness, nor shadow of death, where the workers of iniquity may hide themselves. For he will not lay upon man more than right; that he should enter into judgment with God. [*Job xxxiv.*]

The voice said, Cry. And he said, What shall I cry? All flesh is grass, and all the goodliness thereof is as the flower of the field: the grass withereth, the flower fadeth; because the spirit of the Lord bloweth upon it: surely the people is grass. The grass withereth, the flower fadeth : but the word of our God shall stand forever. [*Isa. xl.*]

A man's heart deviseth his way : but the Lord directeth his steps. [*Prov. xvi.*] For what man is he that can know the counsel of God? or who can think what the will of the Lord is? For the thoughts of mortal men are miserable, and our devices are but uncertain. For the corruptible body presseth down the soul, and the earthy tabernacle weigheth down the mind that museth upon many things. And hardly do we guess aright at things that are upon earth, and with labor do we find the things that are before us : but the things that are in heaven who hath searched out? And thy counsel who hath known, except thou give wisdom and send thy Holy Spirit from above? For so the ways of them which lived on the earth were reformed, and men were taught the things that are pleasing unto thee, and were saved through wisdom. [*Wisdom ix.*]

Lord, make me to know mine end, and the measure of my days, what it is; that I may know how frail I am. Behold, thou hast made my days as a handbreadth; and mine age is as nothing before thee : verily every man at his best state is altogether vanity. Surely every man walketh in a vain show : surely they are disquieted in vain : he heapeth up riches, and knoweth not who shall gather them. And now, Lord, what wait I for? my hope is in thee. Deliver me from all my transgressions. I was dumb, I opened not my mouth ; because thou didst it. Remove thy stroke away from me : I am consumed by the blow of thine hand. When thou with rebukes dost correct man for iniquity, thou makest his beauty to consume away like a moth: surely every man is vanity. Hear my prayer, O Lord, and give ear unto my cry: hold not thy peace at my tears: for I am a stranger with thee, and a sojourner, as all my fathers were. O spare me, that I may recover strength, before I go hence, and be no more. [*Ps. xxxix.*]

THE LIFE OF THE SPIRIT.

There is a spirit in man: and the inspiration of the Almighty giveth them understanding. [*Job xxxii.*]

Jesus said unto her, I am the resurrection, and the life: he that believeth in me, though he were dead, yet shall he live: and whosoever liveth and believeth in me shall never die. [*John xi.*] Verily, verily, I say unto you, He that heareth my word, and believeth on him that sent me, hath eternal life, and shall not come into condemnation; but is passed from death unto life. [*John v.*] For bodily exercise profiteth little: but godliness is profitable unto all things, having promise of the life that now is, and of that which is to come. [*1 Tim. iv.*] In the way of righteousness is life; and in the pathway thereof there is no death. [*Prov. xii.*]

Labor not for the meat which perisheth, but for that meat which endureth unto eternal life, which the Son of man shall give unto you: for him hath God the Father sealed. Verily, verily, I say unto you, Moses gave you not that bread from heaven: but my Father giveth you the true bread from heaven. For the bread of God is he which cometh down from heaven, and giveth life unto the world. Then said they unto him, Lord, evermore give us this bread. And Jesus said unto them, I am the bread of life: he that cometh to me shall never hunger; and he that believeth on me shall never thirst. Verily, verily, I say unto you, He that believeth on me hath everlasting life. I am that bread of life. Your fathers did eat manna in the wilderness, and are dead. This is the bread which cometh down from heaven, that a man may eat thereof, and not die. [*John vi.*]

Jesus answered and said unto her, Whosoever drinketh of this water shall thirst again: but whosoever drinketh of the water that I shall give him shall never thirst; but the water that I shall give him shall be in him a well of water springing up into eternal life. [*John iv.*]

Behold I come quickly; and my reward is with me, to give every man according as his works shall be. I am Alpha and Omega, the beginning and the end, the first and the last. Blessed are they that do his commandments, that they may have right to the tree of life, and may enter in through the gates into the city. And the Spirit and the bride say, Come. And let him that heareth say, Come. And let him that is athirst come. And whosoever will, let him take the water of life freely. [*Rev. xxii.*]

THE DEEP WATERS.

Save me, O God; for the waters are come in unto my soul. I am come into deep waters, where the floods overflow me. [*Ps. lxix.*] The floods have lifted up, O

Lord, the floods have lifted up their voice; the floods lift up their waves. [*Ps. xciii.*] Deep calleth unto deep at the noise of thy waterspouts: all thy waves and thy billows have gone over me. [*Ps. xlii.*] The Lord on high is mightier than the noise of many waters, yea, than the mighty waves of the sea. [*Ps. xciii.*]

O Lord God of my salvation, I have cried day and night before thee: let my prayer come before thee: incline thine ear unto my cry: for my soul is full of troubles: and my life draweth nigh unto the grave. I am counted with them that go down into the pit: I am as a man that hath no strength: mine eye mourneth by reason of affliction: Lord, I have called daily upon thee, I have stretched out my hands unto thee. Wilt thou shew wonders to the dead? shall the dead arise and praise thee? Shall thy loving-kindness be declared in the grave? or thy faithfulness in destruction? Shall thy wonders be known in the dark? and thy righteousness in the land of forgetfulness? But unto thee have I cried, O Lord; and in the morning shall my prayer prevent thee. Lord, why castest thou off my soul? Why hidest thou thy face from me? [*Ps. lxxxviii.*] Hide not thy face from thy servant; for I am in trouble: hear me speedily. [*Ps. lxix.*]

Woe is me for my hurt! my wound is grievous: but I said, Truly this is a grief, and I must bear it. My tabernacle is spoiled, and all my cords are broken: my children are gone forth of me, and they are not: there is none to stretch forth my tent any more, and to set up my curtains. O Lord, I know that the way of man is not in himself: it is not in man that walketh to direct his steps. O Lord, correct me, but with judgment: not in thine anger, lest thou bring me to nothing. [*Jer. x.*]

Is it nothing to you, all ye that pass by? behold, and see if there be any sorrow like unto my sorrow, which is done unto me, wherewith the Lord hath afflicted me. [*Lam. i.*] I am so troubled that I cannot speak. I have considered the days of old, the years of ancient times. I call to remembrance my song in the night: I commune with mine own heart: and my spirit made diligent search. Will the Lord cast off for ever? and will he be favorable no more? Is his mercy clean gone for ever? doth his promise fail for evermore? Hath God forgotten to be gracious? hath he in anger shut up his tender mercies? And I said, This is my infirmity: but I will remember the years of the right hand of the Most High. [*Ps. lxxvii.*]

It is better to go to the house of mourning than to go to the house of feasting: for that is the end of all men; and the living will lay it to his heart. Sorrow is better than laughter: for by the sadness of the countenance the heart is made better. The heart of the wise is in the house of mourning: but the heart of fools is in the house of mirth. In the day of prosperity be joyful, but in the day of adversity consider: God also hath set the one over against the other, to the end that man should find nothing after him. [*Eccl. vii.*]

Although affliction cometh not forth of the dust, neither doth trouble spring out of the ground; yet man is born unto trouble, as the sparks fly upward. [*Job v.*]

SUDDEN DEATH.

Boast not thyself of to-morrow; for thou knowest not what a day may bring forth. [*Prov. xxvii.*] But, beloved, be not ignorant of this one thing, that one day is with the Lord as a thousand years, and a thousand years as one day. The Lord is not slack concerning his promise, as some men count slackness: but is long-suffering to us-ward, not willing that any should perish, but that all should come to repentance. But the day of the Lord will come as a thief in the night: in the which the heavens shall pass away with a great noise, and the elements shall melt with fervent heat, the earth also and the works that are therein shall be burned up. Seeing then that all these things shall be dissolved, what manner of persons ought ye to be in all holy conversation and godliness, looking for and hasting unto the coming of the day of God, wherein the heavens being on fire shall be dissolved, and the elements shall melt with fervent heat? Nevertheless we, according to his promise, look for new heavens and a new earth, wherein dwelleth righteousness. Wherefore, beloved, seeing that ye look for such things, be diligent that ye may be found of him in peace, without spot, and blameless. [*2 Pet. iii.*]

But of that day and hour knoweth no man, no, not the angels of heaven, but my Father only. But as the days of Noah were, so shall also the coming of the Son of man be. For as in the days that were before the flood they were eating and drinking, marrying, and giving in marriage, until the day that Noah entered into the ark, and knew not until the flood came, and took them all away; so shall also the coming of the Son of man be. Then shall two be in the field; the one shall be taken, and the other left. Two women shall be grinding at the mill; the one shall be taken, and the other left. Watch therefore; for ye know not what hour your Lord doth come. But know this, that if the goodman of the house had known in what watch the thief would come, he would have watched, and would not have suffered his house to be broken up. Therefore be ye also ready: for in such an hour as ye think not the Son of man cometh. Who then is a faithful and wise servant, whom his lord hath made ruler over his household, to give them meat in due season? Blessed is that servant, whom his lord when he cometh shall find so doing. Verily I say unto you, that he shall make him ruler over all his goods. [*Matt. xxiv.*]

Go to now, ye that say, To-day or to-morrow, we will go into such a city, and continue there a year, and buy and sell, and get gain. Whereas ye know not what shall be on the morrow. For what is your life? It is even a vapor, that appeareth for a little time, and then vanisheth away. [*Jas. iv.*] Now my days are swifter than a post: they flee away: they are passed away as the swift ships. [*Job ix.*] My days are swifter than a weaver's shuttle. [*Job vii.*] As the Lord liveth and as thy soul liveth, there is but a step between me and death. [*1 Sam. xx.*] Yet I will say of the Lord, He is my refuge and my fortress: my God; in him will I trust. Thou shalt not be afraid for the terror by night; nor for the arrow that flieth by day; nor for the pestilence that walketh in darkness; nor for the destruction that wasteth at noonday. For he shall give his angels charge over thee, to keep thee in all thy ways. [*Ps. xci.*]

I must work the works of him that sent me, while it is day : the night cometh, when no man can work. [*John ix.*] Watch ye therefore : for ye know not when the master of the house cometh, at even, or at midnight, or at the cockcrowing, or in the morning : lest coming suddenly he find you sleeping. And what I say unto you I say unto all, Watch. [*Mark xiii.*]

TRIAL AND SUFFERING.

Blessed is the man that endureth temptation : for when he is tried, he shall receive the crown of life, which the Lord hath promised to them that love him. [*Jas. i.*]

I heard, but I understood not : then said I, O my Lord, what shall be the end of these things? And he said, Go thy way, Daniel : for the words are closed up and sealed till the time of the end. Many shall be purified, and made white, and tried ; but the wicked shall do wickedly : and none of the wicked shall understand ; but the wise shall understand. Blessed is he that waiteth. But go thou thy way till the end be : for thou shalt rest, and stand in thy lot at the end of the days. [*Dan. xii.*]

Then came to him the mother of Zebedee's children with her sons, worshipping him, and desiring a certain thing of him. And he said unto her, What wilt thou? She saith unto him, Grant that these my two sons may sit, the one on thy right hand, and the other on the left, in thy kingdom. But Jesus answered and said, Ye know not what ye ask. Are ye able to drink of the cup that I shall drink of, and to be baptized with the baptism that I am baptized with? They say unto him, We are able. And he saith unto them, Ye shall drink indeed of my cup, and be baptized with the baptism that I am baptized with: but to sit on my right hand, and on my left, is not mine to give, but it shall be given to them for whom it is prepared of my Father. [*Matt. xx.*] For we are laborers together with God: ye are God's husbandry, ye are God's building. According to the grace of God which is given unto me, as a wise masterbuilder, I have laid the foundation, and another buildeth thereon. But let every man take heed how he buildeth thereupon. For other foundation can no man lay than that is laid, which is Jesus Christ. Now if any man build upon this foundation gold, silver, precious stones, wood, hay, stubble; every man's work shall be made manifest: for the day shall declare it, because it shall be revealed by fire; and the fire shall try every man's work of what sort it is. If any man's work abide which he hath built thereupon, he shall receive a reward. If any man's work shall be burned, he shall suffer loss: but he himself shall be saved; yet so as by fire. Know ye not that ye are the temple of God, and that the spirit of God dwelleth in you? If any man defile the temple of God, him shall God destroy; for the temple of God is holy, which temple ye are. [1 *Cor. iii.*]

Behold, I come quickly: hold that fast which thou hast, that no man take thy crown. Him that overcometh will I make a pillar in the temple of my God, and he shall go no more out: and I will write upon him the name of my God, and the name of the city of my God, which is new

Jerusalem, which cometh down out of heaven from my God: and I will write upon him my new name. [*Rev. iii.*] To him that overcometh will I give to eat of the tree of life, which is in the midst of the paradise of God. [*Rev. ii.*]

Wherefore, my beloved, as ye have always obeyed, not as in my presence only, but now much more in my absence, work out your own salvation with fear and trembling: for it is God which worketh in you both to will and to do of his good pleasure. [*Phil. ii.*]

THE WILL OF GOD.

Then cometh Jesus with them unto a place called Gethsemane, and saith unto the disciples. Sit ye here, while I go and pray yonder. And he went a little further, and fell on his face, and prayed, saying, O my Father, if it be possible, let this cup pass from me: nevertheless, not as I will, but as thou wilt. And he cometh unto the disciples, and findeth them asleep, and saith unto Peter, What, could ye not watch with me one hour? Watch and pray, that ye enter not into temptation: the spirit indeed is willing, but the flesh is weak. He went away again the second time, and prayed, saying, O my Father, if this cup may not pass away from me, except I drink it, thy will be done. [*Matt. xxvi.*]

There hath no temptation taken you but such as is common to man: but God is faithful, who will not suffer you to be tempted above that ye are able; but will with the temptation also make a way to escape, that ye may be able to bear it. [1 *Cor. x.*] Beloved, think it not strange concerning the fiery trial which is to try you, as though some strange thing happened unto you: but rejoice, inasmuch as ye are partakers of Christ's sufferings; that, when his glory shall be revealed, ye may be glad also with exceeding joy. [1 *Peter iv.*] Behold, I have refined thee, but not with silver; I have chosen thee in the furnace of affliction. [*Isa. xlviii.*] It is good for me that I have been afflicted; that I might learn thy statutes. [*Ps. cxix.*]

Ye have forgotten the exhortation which speaketh unto you as unto children, My son, despise not thou the chastening of the Lord, nor faint when thou art rebuked of him: for whom the Lord loveth he chasteneth, and scourgeth every son whom he receiveth. If ye endure chastening, God dealeth with you as with sons; for what son is he whom the father chasteneth not? Furthermore, we have had fathers of our flesh which corrected us, and we gave them reverence: shall we not much rather be in subjection unto the Father of spirits, and live? For they verily for a few days chastened us after their own pleasure; but he for our profit, that we might be partakers of his holiness. Now no chastening for the present seemeth to be joyous, but grievous: nevertheless, afterward it yieldeth the peaceable fruit of righteousness unto them which are exercised thereby. Wherefore lift up the hands which hang down, and the feeble knees; and make straight paths for your feet, lest that which is lame be turned out of the way; but let it rather be healed. Follow peace with all men, and holiness, without which no man shall see the Lord. [*Heb. xii.*]

Behold, happy is the man whom God correcteth: therefore despise not thou the chastening of the Almighty: for he maketh sore, and bindeth up: he woundeth and his hands make whole. He shall deliver thee in six troubles: yea, in seven there shall no evil touch thee. In famine he shall redeem thee from death: and in war from the power of the sword. Thou shalt be hid from the scourge of the tongue: neither shalt thou be afraid of destruction when it cometh. [*Job v.*]

My son, if thou come to serve the Lord, prepare thy soul for temptation. Set thy heart aright, and constantly endure. and make not haste in time of trouble. Cleave unto him, and depart not away, that thou mayest be increased at thy last end. Whatsoever is brought upon thee take cheerfully, and be patient when thou art changed to a low estate. For gold is tried in the fire, and acceptable men in the furnace of adversity. Believe in him, and he will help thee; order thy way aright, and trust in him. Ye that fear the Lord, wait for his mercy; and go not aside, lest ye fall. Ye that fear the Lord, believe him; and your reward shall not fail. Ye that fear the Lord, hope for good, and for everlasting joy and mercy. Look at the generations of old, and see; did ever any trust in the Lord, and was confounded? or did any abide in his fear, and was forsaken? or whom did he ever despise, that called upon him? For the Lord is full of compassion and mercy, longsuffering. and very pitiful, and forgiveth sins, and saveth in time of affliction. Woe be to fearful hearts, and faint hands, and the sinner that goeth two ways! Woe unto him that is faint-hearted! for he believeth not; therefore shall he not be defended. Woe unto you that have lost patience! and what will ye do when the Lord shall visit you? They that fear the Lord will not disobey his word; and they that love him will keep his ways. They that fear the Lord will seek that which is well-pleasing unto him; and they that love him shall be filled with the law. They that fear the Lord will prepare their hearts, and humble their souls in his sight, saying, We will fall into the hands of the Lord, and not into the hands of men: for as his majesty is, so is his mercy. [*Ecclus ii.*]

ASPIRATION.

Unto thee, O Lord, do I lift up my soul. O my God, I trust in thee: turn thee unto me, and have mercy upon me; for I am desolate and afflicted. The troubles of my heart are enlarged: O bring thou me out of my distresses. Look upon mine affliction and my pain: and forgive all my sins. O keep my soul, and deliver me: for I put my trust in thee. [*Ps. xxv.*]

Out of the depths have I cried unto thee, O Lord. Lord, hear my voice: let thine ears be attentive to the voice of my supplications. If thou, Lord, shouldest mark iniquities, O Lord, who shall stand? But there is forgiveness with thee, that thou mayest be feared. I wait for the Lord, my soul doth wait, and in his word do I hope. My soul waiteth for the Lord more than they that watch for the morning: yea, more than they that watch for the morning. Let Israel hope in the Lord: for with the Lord there is mercy, and with him is plenteous redemption. And he shall redeem Israel from all his iniquities. [*Ps. cxxx.*]

Have mercy upon me, O God, according to thy lovingkindness: according unto the multitude of thy tender mercies blot out my transgressions. Wash me thoroughly from mine iniquity, and cleanse me from my sin. Create in me a clean heart, O God; and renew a right spirit within me. Cast me not away from thy presence; and take not thy Holy Spirit from me. Restore unto me the joy of thy salvation; and uphold me with thy free Spirit. The sacrifices of God are a broken spirit: a broken and a contrite heart, O God, thou wilt not despise. [*Ps. li.*]

Hear my cry, O God; attend unto my prayer. From the end of the earth will I cry unto thee, when my heart is overwhelmed: lead me to the rock that is higher than I. For thou hast been a shelter for me, and I will trust in the covert of thy wings. [*Ps. lxi.*] Be merciful unto me, O God, be merciful unto me: for my soul trusteth in thee: yea, in the shadow of thy wings will I make my refuge, until these calamities be overpast. [*Ps. lvii.*] O send out thy light and thy truth: let them lead me; let them bring me unto thy holy hill, and to thy tabernacles. [*Ps. xliii.*] Whom have I in heaven but thee? and there is none upon earth that I desire besides thee. My flesh and my heart faileth: but God is the strength of my heart, and my portion for ever. [*Ps. lxxiii.*]

As the hart panteth after the water brooks, so panteth my soul after thee, O God. My soul thirsteth for God, for the living God: when shall I come and appear before God? My tears have been my meat day and night, while they continually say unto me, Where is thy God? When I remember these things, I pour out my soul in me; for I had gone with the multitude, I went with them to the house of God, with the voice of joy and praise, with a multitude that kept holyday. Why art thou cast down, O my soul? and why art thou disquieted in me? hope thou in God: for I shall yet praise him for the help of his countenance. O my God, my soul is cast down within me: therefore will I remember thee. Deep calleth unto deep at the noise of thy waterspouts: all thy waves and thy billows are gone over me. Yet the Lord will command his loving-kindness in the daytime, and in the night his song shall be with me, and my prayer unto the God of my life. [*Ps. xlii.*]

Into thine hand I commit my spirit: thou hast redeemed me, O Lord God of truth. [*Ps. xxxi.*]

GOD OUR COMFORT.

Blessed be God, even the Father of our Lord Jesus Christ, the Father of mercies, and the God of all comfort, who comforteth us in all our tribulation, that we may be able to comfort them which are in any trouble, by the comfort wherewith we ourselves are comforted of God. [*2 Cor. i.*]

Come unto me, all ye that labor and are heavy laden, and I will give you rest. Take my yoke upon you, and learn of me; for I am meek and lowly in heart: and ye shall find rest unto your souls. For my yoke is easy, and my burden is light. [*Matt. xi.*]

Wait on the Lord: be of good courage, and he shall strengthen thine heart: wait, I say, on the Lord. [*Ps. xxvii.*] The Lord hath appeared of old unto me, saying, Yea, I have loved thee with an everlasting love: therefore with loving-kindness have I drawn thee. [*Jer. xxxi.*] For I know the thoughts that I think toward you, saith the Lord, thoughts of peace, and not of evil, to give you hope in your latter end. Then shall ye call upon me, and ye shall go and pray unto me, and I will hearken unto you. And ye shall seek me, and find me, when ye shall search for me with all your heart. [*Jer. xxix.*] As one whom his mother comforteth, so will I comfort you, and ye shall be comforted in Jerusalem. [*Isa. lxvi.*] For the Lord will not cast off for ever: but though he cause grief, yet will he have compassion according to the multitude of his mercies. For he doth not afflict willingly, nor grieve the children of men. [*Lam. iii.*]

If ye love me, keep my commandments. And I will pray the Father, and he shall give you another Comforter, that he may abide with you for ever; even the Spirit of truth; whom the world cannot receive, because it seeth him not, neither knoweth him: but ye know him; for he dwelleth with you, and shall be in you. I will not leave you comfortless; I will come to you. Yet a little while, and the world seeth me no more; but ye see me: because I live, ye shall live also. At that day ye shall know that I am in my Father, and ye in me, and I in you. [*John xiv.*]

The Lord is my light and my salvation; whom shall I fear? the Lord is the strength of my life; of whom shall I be afraid? Though a host should encamp against me, my heart shall not fear: though war should rise against me, in this will I be confident. One thing have I desired of the Lord, that will I seek after; that I may dwell in the house of the Lord all the days of my life, to behold the beauty of the Lord, and to inquire in his temple. For in the time of trouble he shall hide me in his pavilion: in the secret of his tabernacle shall he hide me; he shall set me up upon a rock. And now shall mine head be lifted up above mine enemies round about me: therefore will I offer in his tabernacle sacrifices of joy; I will sing, yea, I will sing praises unto the Lord. Hear, O Lord, when I cry with my voice; have mercy also upon me, and answer me. When thou saidst, Seek ye my face; my heart said unto thee, Thy face, Lord, will I seek. Hide not thy face far from me; put not thy servant away in anger: thou hast been my help; leave me not, neither forsake me, O God of my salvation. When my father and my mother forsake me, then the Lord will take me up. Teach me thy way, O Lord, and lead me in a plain path. I had fainted, unless I had believed to see the goodness of the Lord in the land of the living. [*Ps. xxvii.*]

GOD OUR REFUGE.

God is our refuge and strength, a very present help in trouble. Therefore will not we fear, though the earth be removed, and though the mountains be carried into the midst of the sea; though the waters thereof roar and be troubled, though the mountains shake with the swelling thereof. There is a river, the streams whereof shall make glad the city of God, the holy place of the tabernacles of the Most High. God is in the midst of her; she shall not be moved: God shall help her, and that right early. Be still, and know that I am God: I will be exalted among the heathen, I will be exalted in the earth. The Lord of hosts is with us: the God of Jacob is our refuge. [*Ps. xlvi.*]

The Lord is good, a strong hold in the day of trouble; and he knoweth them that trust in him. [*Nah. i.*] Do not err, my beloved brethren. Every good gift and every perfect gift is from above, and cometh down from the Father of lights, with whom is no variableness, neither shadow of turning. [*Jas. i.*] Truly my soul waiteth upon God: from him cometh my salvation. He only is my rock and my salvation: he is my defence: I shall not be greatly moved. My soul, wait thou only upon God: trust in him at all times; ye people, pour out your heart before him: God is a refuge for us. [*Ps. lxii.*] When the poor and needy seek water, and there is none, and their tongue faileth for thirst, I the Lord will hear them. I the God of Israel will not forsake them. [*Isa. xli.*] O Israel, Fear not: for I have redeemed thee, I have called thee by thy name; thou art mine. When thou passest through the waters, I will be with thee; and through the rivers, they shall not overflow thee: when thou walkest through the fire, thou shalt not be burned; neither shall the flame kindle upon thee. For I am the Lord thy God, the Holy One of Israel, thy Saviour. [*Isa. xliii.*]

Thou wilt keep him in perfect peace, whose mind is stayed on thee: because he trusteth in thee. Trust ye in the Lord for ever: for in the Lord our God is everlasting strength. [*Isa. xxvi.*] It is of the Lord's mercies that we are not consumed, because his compassions fail not. They are new every morning: great is thy faithfulness. The Lord is my portion, saith my soul; therefore will I hope in him. The Lord is good unto them that wait for him, to the soul that seeketh him. It is good that a man should both hope and quietly wait for the salvation of the Lord. [*Lam. iii.*]

Hast thou not known? hast thou not heard, that the everlasting God, the Lord, the Creator of the ends of the earth, fainteth not, neither is weary? there is no searching of his understanding. He giveth power to the faint; and to them that have no might he increaseth strength. Even the youths shall faint and be weary, and the young men shall utterly fall: but they that wait upon the Lord shall renew their strength; they shall mount up with wings as eagles; they shall run, and not be weary; and they shall walk, and not faint. [*Isa. xl.*]

For the whole world before thee is as a little grain of the balance, yea, as a drop of the morning dew that falleth down upon the earth. But thou hast mercy upon all;

thou lovest all the things that are, and abhorrest nothing which thou hast made: for never wouldest thou have made anything, if thou hadst hated it. And how could anything have endured, if it had not been thy will? or been preserved, if not called by thee? But thou sparest all: for they are thine, O Lord, thou lover of souls. [*Wisdom xi.*]

O Lord, thou hast searched me, and known me. Thou knowest my downsitting and mine uprising; thou understandest my thought afar off. Thou compassest my path and my lying down, and art acquainted with all my ways. For there is not a word in my tongue, but, lo, O Lord, thou knowest it altogether. Thou hast beset me behind and before, and laid thine hand upon me. Such knowledge is too wonderful for me; it is high, I cannot attain unto it. Whither shall I go from thy Spirit? or whither shall I flee from thy presence? If I ascend up into heaven, thou art there: if I make my bed in the grave, behold, thou art there. If I take the wings of the morning, and dwell in the uttermost parts of the sea; even there shall thy hand lead me, and thy right hand shall hold me. If I say, Surely the darkness shall cover me; even the night shall be light about me. Yea, the darkness hideth not from thee; but the night shineth as the day: the darkness and the light are both alike to thee [*Ps. cxxxix.*]

He that dwelleth in the secret place of the Most High shall abide under the shadow of the Almighty. I will say of the Lord, He is my refuge and my fortress: my God; in him will I trust. Surely he shall deliver thee from the snare of the fowler, and from the noisome pestilence. He shall cover thee with his feathers, and under his wings shalt thou trust: his truth shall be thy shield and buckler. Thou shalt not be afraid for the terror by night; nor for the arrow that flieth by day: nor for the pestilence that walketh in darkness; nor for the destruction that wasteth at noonday. A thousand shall fall at thy side, and ten thousand at thy right hand; but it shall not come nigh thee. Because thou hast made the Lord, which is my refuge, even the Most High, thy habitation; there shall no evil befall thee, neither shall any plague come nigh thy dwelling. For he shall give his angels charge over thee, to keep thee in all thy ways. They shall bear thee up in their hands, lest thou dash thy foot against a stone. [*Ps. xci.*]

The righteous cry, and the Lord heareth, and delivereth them out of all their troubles. The Lord is nigh unto them that are of a broken heart; and saveth such as be of a contrite spirit. Many are the afflictions of the righteous: but the Lord delivereth him out of them all. The Lord redeemeth the soul of his servants: and none of them that trust in him shall be desolate. [*Ps. xxxiv.*] The Lord looseth the prisoners: the Lord openeth the eyes of the blind: the Lord raiseth them that are bowed down: the Lord loveth the righteous: the Lord preserveth the strangers; he relieveth the fatherless and widow. [*Ps. cxlvi.*] For this God is our God for ever and ever: he will be our guide even unto death. [*Ps. xlviii.*]

The number of a man's days at the most are an hundred years. As a drop of water unto the sea, and a gravelstone in comparison of the sand; so are a thousand years to the days of eternity. Therefore is God patient with them, and poureth forth his mercy upon them. He saw and perceived their end to be evil; therefore he multiplied his compassion. The mercy of man is toward his neighbor; but the mercy of the Lord is upon all flesh: he reproveth, and nurtureth, and teacheth, and bringeth again, as a shepherd his flock. [*Ecclus. xviii.*] They cry unto the Lord in their trouble, and he bringeth them out of their distresses. He maketh the storm a calm, so that the waves thereof are still. Then are they glad because they be quiet: so he bringeth them unto their desired haven. [*Ps. cvii.*]

Ask, and it shall be given unto you; seek, and ye shall find; knock, and it shall be opened unto you: for every one that asketh receiveth; and he that seeketh findeth; and to him that knocketh it shall be opened. Or what man is there of you, whom if his son ask bread, will he give him a stone? Or if he ask a fish, will he give him a serpent? If ye then, being evil, know how to give good gifts unto your children, how much more shall your Father which is in heaven give good things to them that ask him? [*Matt. vii.*] And fear not them which kill the body, but are not able to kill the soul: but rather fear him which is able to destroy both soul and body. Are not two sparrows sold for a farthing? and one of them shall not fall on the ground without your Father. But the very hairs of your head are all numbered. Fear ye not therefore, ye are of more value than many sparrows. [*Matt. x.*]

Therefore I say unto you, Take no thought for your life, what ye shall eat, or what ye shall drink; nor yet for your body, what ye shall put on. Is not the life more than meat, and the body than raiment? Behold the fowls of the air: for they sow not, neither do they reap, nor gather into barns; yet your heavenly Father feedeth them. Are ye not much better than they? Which of you by taking thought can add one cubit unto his stature? And why take ye thought for raiment? Consider the lilies of the field, how they grow; they toil not, neither do they spin: and yet I say unto you, that even Solomon in all his glory was not arrayed like one of these. Wherefore, if God so clothe the grass of the field, which to-day is, and to-morrow is cast into the oven, shall he not much more clothe you, O ye of little faith? [*Matt. vi.*]

The Lord is my shepherd; I shall not want. He maketh me to lie down in green pastures: he leadeth me beside the still waters. He restoreth my soul: he leadeth me in the paths of righteousness for his name's sake. Yea, though I walk through the valley of the shadow of death, I will fear no evil: for thou art with me; thy rod and thy staff they comfort me. Thou preparest a table before me in the presence of mine enemies: thou anointest my head with oil; my cup runneth over. Surely goodness and mercy shall follow me all the days of my life: and I will dwell in the house of the Lord for ever. [*Ps. xxiii.*]

THE FRUIT OF THE SPIRIT.

So is the kingdom of God, as if a man should cast seed into the ground; and should sleep, and rise night and day, and the seed should spring and grow up, he knoweth not how. For the earth bringeth forth fruit of herself; first the blade, then the ear, after that the full corn in the ear. [*Mark iv.*] But the fruit of the Spirit is love, joy, peace, long-suffering, gentleness, goodness, faith, meekness, temperance: against such there is no law. And they that are Christ's have crucified the flesh with the affections and lusts. If we live in the Spirit, let us also walk in the Spirit. [*Gal. v.*] Be not deceived; God is not mocked: for whatsoever a man soweth, that shall he also reap. For he that soweth to his flesh, shall of the flesh reap corruption; but he that soweth to the Spirit shall of the Spirit reap life everlasting. And let us not be weary in well doing: for in due season we shall reap, if we faint not. [*Gal. vi.*]

UPRIGHTNESS AND FIDELITY.

Lord, who shall abide in thy tabernacle? who shall dwell in thy holy hill? He that walketh uprightly, and worketh righteousness, and speaketh the truth in his heart. He that backbiteth not with his tongue, nor doeth evil to his neighbor, nor taketh up a reproach against his neighbor. In whose eyes a vile person is contemned; but he honoreth them that fear the Lord. He that sweareth to his own hurt, and changeth not, nor taketh reward against the innocent. He that doeth these things shall never be moved. [*Ps. xv.*]

Who shall ascend into the hill of the Lord? or who shall stand in his holy place? He that hath clean hands, and a pure heart; who hath not lifted up his soul unto vanity, nor sworn deceitfully. He shall receive a blessing from the Lord, and righteousness from the God of his salvation. This is the generation of them that seek him, that seek thy face, O God of Jacob. Lift up your heads, O ye gates; and be ye lifted up, ye everlasting doors; and the King of glory shall come in. Who is this King of glory? The Lord of hosts, he is the King of glory. [*Ps. xxiv.*]

The steps of a good man are ordered by the Lord: and he delighteth in his way. Though he fall, he shall not be utterly cast down: for the Lord upholdeth him with his hand. I have been young, and now am old; yet have I not seen the righteous forsaken, nor his seed begging bread. Mark the perfect man, and behold the upright: for the end of that man is peace. [*Ps. xxxvii.*]

These are the things that ye shall do; speak ye every man the truth to his neighbor; execute the judgment of truth and peace in your gates: and let none of you imagine evil in your hearts against his neighbor; and love no false oath: for all these are things that I hate, saith the Lord. [*Zech. viii.*] Execute true judgment, and shew mercy and compassion every man to his brother. [*Zech. vii.*]

Enter ye in at the strait gate: for wide is the gate, and broad is the way, that leadeth to destruction, and many there be which go in thereat: because strait is the gate, and narrow is the way, which leadeth unto life, and few there be that find it. Not every one that saith unto me, Lord, Lord, shall enter into the kingdom of heaven; but he that doeth the will of my Father which is in heaven. Therefore, whosoever heareth these sayings of mine and doeth them, I will liken him unto a wise man, which built his house upon a rock: and the rain descended, and the floods came, and the winds blew, and beat upon that house; and it fell not: for it was founded upon a rock. And every one that heareth these sayings of mine, and doeth them not, shall be likened unto a foolish man, which built his house upon the sand: and the rain descended, and the floods came, and the winds blew, and beat upon that house; and it fell: and great was the fall of it. [*Matt. vii.*]

Who then is a faithful and wise servant, whom his lord hath made ruler over his household, to give them meat in due season? Blessed is that servant, whom his lord when he cometh shall find so doing. [*Matt. xxiv.*]

Beware of false prophets, which come to you in sheep's clothing, but inwardly they are ravening wolves. Ye shall know them by their fruits. Do men gather grapes of thorns, or figs of thistles? Even so every good tree bringeth forth good fruit; but a corrupt tree bringeth forth evil fruit. A good tree cannot bring forth evil fruit, neither can a corrupt tree bring forth good fruit. Every tree that bringeth not forth good fruit is hewn down, and cast into the fire. Wherefore by their fruits ye shall know them. [*Matt. vii.*] For whosoever shall do the will of my Father which is in heaven, the same is my brother, and sister, and mother. [*Matt. xii.*]

I know thy works, and charity, and service, and faith, and thy patience, and thy works; and the last to be more than the first. [*Rev. ii.*] Well done, thou good and faithful servant: thou hast been faithful over a few things, I will make thee ruler over many things: enter thou into the joy of thy Lord. [*Matt. xxv.*]

Blessed is the man that walketh not in the counsel of the ungodly, nor standeth in the way of sinners, nor sitteth in the seat of the scornful. But his delight is in the law of the Lord; and in his law doth he meditate day and night. And he shall be like a tree planted by the rivers of water, that bringeth forth his fruit in his season; his leaf also shall not wither; and whatsoever he doeth shall prosper. [*Ps. i.*]

What things were gain to me, those I counted loss for Christ. Yea doubtless, and I count all things but loss for the excellency of the knowledge of Christ Jesus my Lord: for whom I have suffered the loss of all things, and do count them but refuse, that I may win Christ, and be found in him, not having mine own righteousness, which is of the law, but that which is through the faith of Christ, the righteousness which is of God by faith: that I may know him, and the power of his resurrection, and the fellowship of his sufferings, being made conformable unto his death; if by any means I might attain unto the resurrection of the dead. Not as though I had already attained, either were already perfect: but I follow after, if that I may apprehend that for which also I am apprehended of Christ Jesus. Brethren, I count not myself to have apprehended: but this one thing I do, forgetting those things which are behind, and reaching forth unto those things which are before, I press toward the mark for the prize of the high calling of God in Christ Jesus. [*Phil. iii.*]

Finally, brethren, whatsoever things are true, whatsoever things are honest, whatsoever things are just, whatsoever things are pure, whatsoever things are lovely, whatsoever things are of good report; if there be any virtue, and if there be any praise, think on these things. [*Phil. iv.*] For the memorial of virtue is immortal: because it is known with God, and with men. When it is present, men take example at it; and when it is gone, they desire it: it weareth a crown, and triumpheth for ever, having gotten the victory, striving for undefiled rewards. [*Wisdom iv.*]

Let us hear the conclusion of the whole matter: fear God, and keep his commandments: for this is the whole duty of man. For God shall bring every work into judgment, with every secret thing, whether it be good, or whether it be evil. [*Eccl. xii.*]

WISDOM AND WORTH.

Know ye not that there is a prince and a great man fallen this day in Israel? [*2 Sam. iii.*] For, behold, the Lord, the Lord of hosts, doth take away from Jerusalem and from Judah the stay and the staff, the whole stay of bread, and the whole stay of water, the mighty man, and the man of war, the judge, and the prophet, and the prudent, and the ancient, the captain of fifty, and the honorable man, and the counsellor, and the cunning artificer, and the eloquent orator. [*Isa. iii.*] In a moment shall they die, and the people shall be troubled at midnight, and pass away: and the mighty shall be taken away without hand. [*Job xxxiv.*] There is no king saved by the multitude of a host: a mighty man is not delivered by great strength. [*Ps. xxxiii.*] All ye that are about him, bemoan him, and all ye that know his name, say, How is the strong staff broken, and the beautiful rod! [*Jer. xlviii.*]

And David lamented with this lamentation: The beauty of Israel is slain upon thy high places: how are the mighty fallen! Ye mountains of Gilboa, let there be no dew, neither let there be rain, upon you, nor fields of offerings: for there the shield of the mighty is vilely cast away, the shield of Saul, as though he had not been anointed with oil. How are the mighty fallen in the midst of the battle! How are the mighty fallen, and the weapons of war perished! [*2 Sam. i.*]

Let us now praise famous men, and our fathers that begat us. The Lord hath wrought great glory by them through his great power from the beginning. Such as did bear rule in their kingdoms, men renowned for their power, giving counsel by their understanding, and declaring prophecies: leaders of the people by their counsels, and by their knowledge of learning meet for the people, wise and eloquent in their instructions: such as found out musical tunes, and recited verses in writing: rich men furnished with ability, living peaceably in their habitations: all these were honored in their generations, and were the glory of their times. There be of them, that have left a name behind them, that their praises might be reported. And some there be, which have no memorial; who are perished, as though they had never been; and are become as though they had never been born; and their children after them. But these were merciful men, whose righteousness hath not been forgotten. With their seed shall continually remain a good inheritance, and their children are within the covenant. Their seed standeth fast, and their children for their sakes. Their seed shall remain for ever, and their glory shall not be blotted out. Their bodies are buried in peace; but their name liveth for evermore. The people will tell of their wisdom, and the congregation will shew forth their praise. [*Ecclus. xliv.*]

Moreover Job continued his parable, and said: When I went out to the gate through the city, when I prepared my seat in the street, the young men saw me, and hid themselves, and the aged arose, and stood up. The princes refrained talking, and laid their hand on their mouth. The nobles held their peace, and their tongue cleaved to the roof of their mouth. When the ear heard me, then it blessed me: and when the eye saw me, it gave witness to me: because I delivered the poor that cried, and the fatherless, and him that had none to help him. The blessing of him that was ready to perish came upon me; and I caused the widow's heart to sing for joy. I put on righteousness, and it clothed me; my judgment was as a robe and a diadem. I was eyes to the blind, and feet was I to the lame. I was a father to the poor: and the cause which I knew not I searched out. And I brake the jaws of the wicked, and plucked the spoil out of his teeth. Then I said, I shall die in my nest, and I shall multiply my days as the sand. My root was spread out by the waters, and the dew lay all night upon my branch. My glory was fresh in me, and my bow was renewed in my hand. Unto me men gave ear, and waited, and kept silence at my counsel. After my words they spake not again; and my speech dropped upon them. And they waited for me as for the rain; and they opened their mouth wide as for the latter rain. If I laughed on them, they believed it not: and the light of my countenance they cast not down. I chose out their way, and sat chief, and dwelt as a king in the army, as one that comforteth the mourners. [*Job xxix.*]

Blessed be the name of God for ever and ever: for wisdom and might are his: and he changeth the times and the seasons: he removeth kings, and setteth up kings: he giveth wisdom unto the wise, and knowledge to them that know understanding: he revealeth the deep and secret things: he knoweth what is in the darkness, and the light dwelleth with him. [*Dan. ii.*]

He that giveth his mind to the law of the Most High, and is occupied in the meditation thereof, will seek out the wisdom of all the ancient, and be occupied in prophecies. He will keep the sayings of the renowned men: and where subtile parables are, he will be there also. He will seek out the secrets of grave sentences, and be conversant in dark parables. He shall serve among great men, and appear before princes: he will travel through strange countries; for he hath tried the good and the evil among men. He will give his heart to resort early to the Lord that made him, and will pray before the Most

High, and will open his mouth in prayer, and make supplication for his sins. When the great Lord will, he shall be filled with the spirit of understanding: he shall pour out wise sentences, and give thanks unto the Lord in his prayer. He shall direct his counsel and knowledge, and in his secrets shall he meditate. He shall shew forth that which he hath learned, and shall glory in the law of the covenant of the Lord. Many shall commend his understanding; and so long as the world endureth, it shall not be blotted out; his memorial shall not depart away, and his name shall live from generation to generation. Nations shall shew forth his wisdom, and the congregation shall declare his praise. If he die, he shall leave a greater name than a thousand: and if he live, he shall increase it. [*Ecclus. xxxix.*]

The fear of the Lord is the beginning of wisdom: and the knowledge of the Holy One is understanding. [*Prov. ix.*] And unto man he said, Behold, the fear of the Lord, that is wisdom; and to depart from evil is understanding. [*Job xxviii.*]

Happy is the man that findeth wisdom, and the man that getteth understanding: for the merchandise of it is better than the merchandise of silver, and the gain thereof than fine gold. She is more precious than rubies: and all the things thou canst desire are not to be compared unto her. Length of days is in her right hand; and in her left hand riches and honor. Her ways are ways of pleasantness, and all her paths are peace. She is a tree of life to them that lay hold upon her; and happy is every one that retaineth her. My son, keep sound wisdom and discretion: so shall they be life unto thy soul, and grace to thy neck. Then shalt thou walk in thy way safely, and thy foot shall not stumble. When thou liest down, thou shalt not be afraid: yea, thou shalt lie down, and thy sleep shall be sweet. Be not afraid of sudden fear, neither of the desolation of the wicked, when it cometh. For the Lord shall be thy confidence, and shall keep thy foot from being taken. [*Prov. iii.*]

Hear, ye children, the instruction of a father, and attend to know understanding. For I give you good doctrine, forsake ye not my law. For I was my father's son, tender and only beloved in the sight of my mother. He taught me also, and said unto me, Let thine heart retain my words: keep my commandments, and live. Get wisdom, get understanding: forget it not; neither decline from the words of my mouth. Forsake her not, and she shall preserve thee: love her, and she shall keep thee. Wisdom is the principal thing; therefore get wisdom: and with all thy getting get understanding. Exalt her, and she shall promote thee: she shall bring thee to honor, when thou dost embrace her. She shall give to thine head an ornament of grace: a crown of glory shall she deliver to thee. Hear, O my son, and receive my sayings; and the years of thy life shall be many. I have taught thee in the way of wisdom; I have led thee in right paths. When thou goest, thy steps shall not be straitened; and when thou runnest, thou shalt not stumble. Take fast hold of instruction; let her not go: keep her; for she is thy life. [*Prov. iv.*]

For wisdom, which is the worker of all things, taught

me: for in her is an understanding spirit, holy, one only, manifold, subtile, lively, clear, undefiled, plain, not subject to hurt, loving the thing that is good, quick, which cannot be letted, ready to do good, kind to man, steadfast, sure, free from care, having all power, overseeing all things, and going through all understanding, pure, and most subtile, spirits. For wisdom is more moving than any motion: she passeth and goeth through all things by reason of her pureness. For she is the breath of the power of God, and a pure influence flowing from the glory of the Almighty: therefore can no defiled thing fall into her. For she is the brightness of the everlasting light, the unspotted mirror of the power of God, and the image of his goodness. And being but one, she can do all things: and remaining in her she maketh all things new: and in all ages entering into holy souls, she maketh them friends of God, and prophets. For God loveth none but him that dwelleth with wisdom. For she is more beautiful than the sun, and above all the order of the stars: being compared with the light, she is found before it. For after this cometh night: but vice shall not prevail against wisdom. [*Wisdom vii.*]

Unto you therefore, O kings, do I speak, that ye may learn wisdom, and not fall away. For they that keep holiness holily shall be judged holy: and they that have learned such things shall find what to answer. Wherefore set your affection upon my words; desire them, and ye shall be instructed. Wisdom is glorious, and never fadeth away: yea, she is easily seen of them that love her, and found of such as seek her. Whoso seeketh her early shall have no great travail: for he shall find her sitting at his doors. To think therefore upon her is perfection of wisdom: and whoso watcheth for her shall quickly be without care. For she goeth about seeking such as are worthy of her, sheweth herself favorably unto them in the ways and meeteth them in every thought. For the very true beginning of her is the desire of discipline, and the care of discipline is love; and love is the keeping of her laws; and the giving heed unto her laws is the assurance of incorruption; and incorruption maketh us near unto God: therefore the desire of wisdom bringeth to a kingdom. [*Wisdom vi.*]

And the child Samuel ministered unto the Lord before Eli. And the word of the Lord was precious in those days; there was no open vision. And it came to pass at that time, when Eli was laid down in his place, and his eyes began to wax dim, that he could not see; and ere the lamp of God went out in the temple of the Lord, where the ark of God was, and Samuel was laid down to sleep; that the Lord called Samuel: and he answered, Here am I. And he ran unto Eli, and said, Here am I; for thou calledst me. And he said, I called not; lie down again. And he went and lay down. And the Lord called yet again, Samuel. And Samuel arose and went to Eli, and said, Here am I; for thou didst call me. And he answered, I called not, my son; lie down again. And the Lord called Samuel again the third time. And he arose and went to Eli, and said, Here am I; for thou didst call me. And Eli perceived that the Lord had called the child. Therefore Eli said unto Samuel, Go, lie down; and it shall be, if he call thee, that thou shalt say, Speak, Lord; for thy servant heareth. So Samuel went and lay down in his place. And the Lord came, and stood, and called as at other times, Samuel, Samuel. Then Samuel answered, Speak; for thy servant heareth. [*1 Sam. iii.*]

How beautiful upon the mountains are the feet of him that bringeth good tidings, that publisheth peace; that bringeth good tidings of good, that publisheth salvation; that saith unto Zion, Thy God reigneth! [*Isa. lii.*]

Behold my servant, whom I uphold; mine elect, in whom my soul delighteth; I have put my Spirit upon him: he shall bring forth judgment to the Gentiles. He shall not cry, nor lift up, nor cause his voice to be heard in the street. A bruised reed shall he not break, and the smoking flax shall he not quench: he shall bring forth judgment unto truth. He shall not fail nor be discouraged, till he have set judgment in the earth: and the isles shall wait for his law. Thus saith God the Lord, he that created the heavens, and stretched them out; he that spread forth the earth, and that which cometh out of it; he that giveth breath unto the people upon it, and spirit to them that walk therein: I the Lord have called thee in righteousness, and will hold thine hand, and will keep thee, and give thee for a covenant of the people, for a light of the Gentiles; to open the blind eyes, to bring out the prisoners from the prison, and them that sit in darkness out of the prison house. [*Isa. xlii.*]

The spirit of the Lord God is upon me; because the Lord hath anointed me to preach good tidings unto the meek; he hath sent me to bind up the broken-hearted, to proclaim liberty to the captives, and the opening of the prison to them that are bound; to proclaim the acceptable year of the Lord, to comfort all that mourn; to appoint unto them that mourn in Zion, to give unto them beauty for ashes, the oil of joy for mourning, the garment of praise for the spirit of heaviness; that they might be called trees of righteousness, the planting of the Lord, that he might be glorified. [*Isa. lxi.*]

This man was instructed in the way of the Lord; and being fervent in the spirit, he spake and taught diligently the things of the Lord. [*Acts xviii.*] For he was a good man, and full of the Holy Spirit and of faith: and much people was added unto the Lord. [*Acts xi.*] And moreover, because the Preacher was wise, he still taught the people knowledge; yea, he gave good heed, and sought out, and set in order many proverbs. The Preacher sought to find out acceptable words, and that which was written uprightly, even words of truth. [*Eccl. xii.*]

He that speaketh truth sheweth forth righteousness: but a false witness deceit. There is that speaketh like the piercings of a sword: but the tongue of the wise is health. The lip of truth shall be established for ever: but a lying tongue is but for a moment. Deceit is in the heart of them that imagine evil; but to the counsellors of peace is joy. [*Prov. xii.*] The steps of a good man are ordered by the Lord: and he delighteth in his way. Though he fall, he shall not be utterly cast down: for the Lord upholdeth him with his hand. The righteous shall inherit the land, and dwell therein for ever. The mouth of the righteous speaketh wisdom, and his tongue talketh of judgment. The law of his God is in his heart; none of his steps shall slide. [*Ps. xxxvii.*]

The fruit of the righteous is a tree of life; and he that winneth souls is wise. [*Prov. xi.*] And they that be wise shall shine as the brightness of the firmament; and they that turn many to righteousness, as the stars for ever and ever. [*Dan xii.*] And when the chief Shepherd shall appear, ye shall receive a crown of glory that fadeth not away. [*1 Peter v.*] Mark the perfect man, and behold the upright: for the end of that man is peace. [*Ps. xxxvii.*]

Blessed is that man that maketh the Lord his trust, and that respecteth not the proud, nor such as turn aside to lies. Many, O Lord, my God, are thy wonderful works which thou hast done, and thy thoughts which are to us-ward: they cannot be reckoned up in order unto thee: if I would declare and speak of them, they are more than can be numbered. Sacrifice and offering thou didst not desire; burnt offering and sin offering hast thou not required. Then said I, Lo, I come: in the volume of the book it is written of me, I delight to do thy will, O my God: yea, thy law is within my heart. I have preached righteousness in the great congregation: lo, I have not refrained my lips, O Lord, thou knowest. I have not hid thy righteousness within my heart; I have declared thy faithfulness and thy salvation: I have not concealed thy loving-kindness and thy truth from the great congregation. Withhold not thou thy tender mercies from me, O Lord: let thy loving-kindness and thy truth continually preserve me. Let all those that seek thee, rejoice and be glad in thee: let such as love thy salvation say continually, The Lord be magnified. [*Ps. xl.*]

PATIENCE.

Therefore being justified by faith, we have peace with God through our Lord Jesus Christ: by whom also we have access by faith into this grace wherein we stand, and rejoice in hope of the glory of God. And not only so, but we glory in tribulations also; knowing that tribulation worketh patience; and patience, experience; and experience, hope: and hope maketh not ashamed; because the love of God is shed abroad in our hearts by the Holy Spirit which is given unto us. [*Rom. v.*] For this is thankworthy, if a man for conscience toward God endure grief, suffering wrongfully. For what glory is it, if, when ye be buffeted for your faults, ye shall take it patiently? but if, when ye do well, and suffer for it, ye take it patiently, this is acceptable with God. For even hereunto were ye called: because Christ also suffered for you, leaving you an example, that ye should follow his steps. [*1 Peter ii.*]

We then, as workers together with him, beseech you also that ye receive not the grace of God in vain. But in all things approving ourselves as the ministers of God, in much patience, in afflictions, in necessities, in distresses, in stripes, in imprisonments, in tumults, in labors, in watchings, in fastings; by pureness, by knowledge, by long-suffering, by kindness, by the Holy Spirit, by love unfeigned, by the word of truth, by the power of God, by the armor of righteousness on the right hand and on the left, by honor and dishonor, by evil report and good report: as deceivers, and yet true; as unknown, and yet well known; as dying, and, behold, we live; as chastened, and not killed; as sorrowful, yet always rejoicing; as poor, yet making many rich; as having nothing, and yet possessing all things. [*2 Cor. vi.*]

Surely he hath borne our griefs, and carried our sorrows; yet we did esteem him stricken, smitten of God, and afflicted. But he was wounded for our transgressions, he was bruised for our iniquities: the chastisement of our peace was upon him; and with his stripes we are healed. [*Isa. liii.*]

Be patient therefore, brethren, unto the coming of the Lord. Behold, the husbandman waiteth for the precious fruit of the earth, and hath long patience for it, until he receive the early and latter rain. Be ye also patient, stablish your hearts: for the coming of the Lord draweth nigh. Murmur not one against another, brethren, lest ye be condemned: behold, the judge standeth before the door. Take, my brethren, the prophets, who have spoken in the name of the Lord, for an example of suffering, affliction, and patience. Behold, we count them happy which endure. Ye have heard of the patience of Job, and have seen the end of the Lord; that the Lord is very pitiful, and of tender mercy. [*Jas. v.*] For God is not unrighteous to forget your work and labor of love, which ye have shewed toward his name, in that ye have ministered to the saints, and do minister. And we desire that every one of you do shew the same diligence to the full assurance of hope unto the end: that ye be not slothful, but followers of them who through faith and patience inherit the promises. [*Heb. vi.*] Better is the end of a thing than the beginning thereof: and the patient in spirit is better than the proud in spirit. [*Eccl. vii.*]

Wherefore, seeing we also are compassed about with so great a cloud of witnesses, let us lay aside every weight, and the sin which doth so easily beset us, and let us run with patience the race that is set before us, looking unto Jesus the author and finisher of our faith; who for the joy that was set before him endured the cross, despising the shame, and is set down at the right hand of the throne of God. For consider him that endured such contradiction of sinners against himself, lest ye be wearied and faint in your minds. Ye have not yet resisted unto blood, striving against sin. [*Heb. xii.*]

Now the God of patience and consolation grant you to be likeminded one toward another according to Christ Jesus: that ye may with one mind and one mouth glorify God, even the Father of our Lord Jesus Christ. [*Rom. xv.*]

GENTLENESS AND LOVE.

When he giveth quietness, who then can make trouble? [*Job xxxiv.*] For thus saith the Lord God, the Holy One of Israel; In returning and rest shall ye be saved; in quietness and in confidence shall be your strength. [*Isa. xxx.*] And the work of righteousness shall be peace; and the effect of righteousness, quietness and assurance for ever. And my people shall dwell in a peaceable habitation, and in sure dwellings, and in quiet resting places. [*Isa. xxxii.*] But let it be the hidden man of the heart, in that which is not corruptible, even the ornament of a meek and quiet spirit, which is in the sight of God of great price. [*1 Peter iii.*]

Who is a wise man and endued with knowledge among you? let him shew out of a good conversation his works with meekness of wisdom. But if ye have bitter envying and strife in your hearts, glory not, and lie not against the truth. This wisdom descendeth not from above, but is earthly, sensual, devilish. For where envying and strife is, there is confusion and every evil work. But the wisdom that is from above is first pure, then peaceable, gentle, and easy to be entreated, full of mercy and good fruits, without partiality, and without hypocrisy. And the fruit of righteousness is sown in peace for them that make peace. [*Jas. iii.*]

Herein is my Father glorified, that ye bear much fruit; so shall ye be my disciples. As the Father hath loved me, so have I loved you: continue ye in my love. If ye keep my commandments, ye shall abide in my love; even as I have kept my Father's commandments, and abide in his love. These things have I spoken unto you, that my joy might remain in you, and that your joy might be full. This is my commandment, that ye love one another, as I have loved you. Greater love hath no man than this, that a man lay down his life for his friends. Ye are my friends, if ye do whatsoever I command you. Henceforth I call you not servants; for the servant knoweth not what his lord doeth: but I have called you friends. [*John xv.*]

And we have known and believed the love that God

hath to us. God is love; and he that dwelleth in love dwelleth in God, and God in him. Herein is our love made perfect, that we may have boldness in the day of judgment: because as he is, so are we in this world. There is no fear in love; but perfect love casteth out fear: because fear hath torment. He that feareth is not made perfect in love. We love him, because he first loved us. If a man say, I love God, and hateth his brother, he is a liar: for he that loveth not his brother whom he hath seen, how can he love God whom he hath not seen? And this commandment have we from him, that he who loveth God love his brother also. [*1 John iv.*]

He that findeth his life shall lose it: and he that loseth his life for my sake shall find it. He that receiveth you receiveth me; and he that receiveth me receiveth him that sent me. He that receiveth a prophet in the name of a prophet shall receive a prophet's reward; and he that receiveth a righteous man in the name of a righteous man shall receive a righteous man's reward. And whosoever shall give to drink unto one of these little ones a cup of cold water only in the name of a disciple, verily I say unto you, he shall in no wise lose his reward. [*Matt. x.*]

Though I speak with the tongues of men and of angels, and have not charity, I am become as sounding brass, or a tinkling cymbal. And though I have the gift of prophecy, and understand all mysteries, and all knowledge; and though I have all faith, so that I could remove mountains, and have not charity, I am nothing. And though I bestow all my goods to feed the poor, and though I give my body to be burned, and have not charity, it profiteth me nothing. Charity suffereth long, and is kind; charity envieth not; charity vaunteth not itself, is not puffed up, doth not behave itself unseemly, seeketh not her own, is not easily provoked, thinketh no evil; rejoiceth not in iniquity, but rejoiceth in the truth; beareth all things, believeth all things, hopeth all things, endureth all things. Charity never faileth; but whether there be prophecies, they shall fail; whether there be tongues, they shall cease; whether there be knowledge, it shall vanish away. And now abideth faith, hope, charity, these three; but the greatest of these is charity. [*1 Cor. xiii.*]

Therefore all things whatsoever ye would that men should do to you, do ye even so to them: for this is the law and the prophets. [*Matt. vii.*] There is that maketh himself rich, yet hath nothing: there is that maketh himself poor, yet hath great riches. [*Prov. xiii.*] He that oppresseth the poor reproacheth his Maker: but he that honoreth him hath mercy on the poor. He that despiseth his neighbor sinneth: but he that hath mercy on the poor, happy is he. [*Prov. xiv.*] Is not this the fast that I have chosen? to loose the bands of wickedness, to undo the heavy burdens, and to let the oppressed go free, and that ye break every yoke? Is it not to deal thy bread to the hungry, and that thou bring the poor that are cast out to thy house? when thou seest the naked, that thou cover him; and that thou hide not thyself from thine own flesh? [*Isa. lviii.*]

And Jesus sat over against the treasury, and beheld

how the people cast money into the treasury: and many that were rich cast in much. And there came a certain poor widow, and she threw in two mites, which make a farthing. And he called unto him his disciples, and saith unto them, Verily I say unto you, that this poor widow hath cast more in, than all they which have cast into the treasury: for all they did cast in of their abundance; but she of her want did cast in all that she had, even all her living. [*Mark xii.*]

Then shall the King say, Come, ye blessed of my Father, inherit the kingdom prepared for you from the foundation of the world: for I was a hungered, and ye gave me meat: I was thirsty, and ye gave me drink: I was a stranger, and ye took me in: naked, and ye clothed me: I was sick, and ye visited me: I was in prison, and ye came unto me. Then shall the righteous answer him, saying, Lord, when saw we thee a hungered, and fed thee? or thirsty, and gave thee drink?
And the King shall answer and say unto them, Verily I say unto you, Inasmuch as ye have done it unto one of the least of these my brethren, ye have done it unto me. [*Matt. xxv.*]

FRIENDSHIP.

Change not a friend for any good by no means; neither a faithful brother for the gold of Ophir. Forego not a wise and good woman: for her grace is above gold. [*Ecclus. vii.*]
And Ruth said, Entreat me not to leave thee, or to

return from following after thee: for whither thou goest, I will go: and where thou lodgest, I will lodge: thy people shall be my people, and thy God my God: where thou diest, will I die, and there will I be buried: the Lord do so to me, and more also, if aught but death part thee and me. [*Ruth i.*]

And it came to pass, that the soul of Jonathan was knit with the soul of David, and Jonathan loved him as his own soul. Then Jonathan and David made a covenant, because he loved him as his own soul. And Jonathan stripped himself of the robe that was upon him, and gave it to David, and his garments, even to his sword, and to his bow, and to his girdle. [*1 Sam. xviii.*)

And David lamented with this lamentation over Saul and over Jonathan his son: The beauty of Israel is slain upon thy high places: how are the mighty fallen! Ye mountains of Gilboa, let there be no dew, neither let there be rain, upon you, nor fields of offerings: for there the shield of the mighty is vilely cast away, the shield of Saul, as though he had not been anointed with oil. From the blood of the slain, from the fat of the mighty, the bow of Jonathan turned not back, and the sword of Saul returned not empty. Saul and Jonathan were lovely and pleasant in their lives, and in their death they were not divided; they were swifter than eagles, they were stronger than lions. Ye daughters of Israel, weep over Saul. How are the mighty fallen in the midst of battle! O Jonathan, thou wast slain in thine high places. I am distressed for thee, my brother Jonathan: very pleasant hast thou been unto me: thy love to me was wonderful, passing the love of women. How are the mighty fallen, and the weapons of war perished! [*2 Sam. i.*]

PURITY AND HUMILITY.

Blessed are the pure in heart: for they shall see God. [*Matt. v.*] He that loveth pureness of heart, for the grace of his lips the king shall be his friend. [*Prov. xxii.*] Pure religion and undefiled before our God and Father is this, to visit the fatherless and widows in their affliction, and to keep himself unspotted from the world. [*Jas. i.*]

Though the Lord be high, yet hath he respect unto the lowly: but the proud he knoweth afar off. [*Ps. cxxxviii.*] He hath shewed strength with his arm; he hath scattered the proud in the imagination of their hearts. He hath put down the mighty from their seats, and exalted them of low degree. [*Luke i.*] The fear of the Lord is the instruction of wisdom; and before honor is humility. [*Prov. xv.*] By humility and the fear of the Lord are riches and honor and life. [*Prov. xxii.*]

And he spake this parable unto certain which trusted in themselves that they were righteous, and despised others: Two men went up into the temple to pray; the one a Pharisee, and the other a publican. The Pharisee stood and prayed thus with himself, God, I thank thee that I am not as other men are, extortioners, unjust, adulterers, or even as this publican. I fast twice in the week, I give tithes of all that I possess. And the publican, standing afar off, would not lift up so much as his eyes unto heaven, but smote upon his breast, saying, God be merciful to me a sinner. I tell you, this man went down to his house justified rather than the other: for every one that exalteth himself shall be abased; and he that humbleth himself shall be exalted. [*Luke xviii.*]

Take heed that ye do not your alms before men, to be seen of them: otherwise ye have no reward of your Father which is in heaven. Therefore when thou doest thine alms, do not sound a trumpet before thee, as the hypocrites do in the synagogues and in the streets, that they may have glory of men. Verily I say unto you, They have their reward. But when thou doest alms, let not thy left hand know what thy right hand doeth. [*Matt. vi.*] And when thou prayest, thou shalt not be as the hypocrites are: for they love to pray standing in the synagogues and in the corners of the streets, that they may be seen of men. Verily I say unto you, They have their reward. But thou, when thou prayest, enter into thy closet, and when thou hast shut thy door, pray to thy Father which is in secret; and thy Father which seeth in secret shall reward thee openly. But when ye pray, use not vain repetitions, as the heathen do: for they think that they shall be heard for their much speaking. Be not ye therefore like unto them: for your Father knoweth what things ye have need of, before ye ask him. [*Matt. vi.*] But the hour cometh, and now is, when the true worshippers shall worship the Father in spirit and in truth: for the Father seeketh such to worship him. God is a Spirit, and they that worship him must worship him in spirit and in truth. [*John iv.*]

JOY AND FAITH.

And seeing the multitudes, Jesus went up into a mountain: and when he was set, his disciples came unto him: and he opened his mouth, and taught them, saying, Blessed are the poor in spirit: for theirs is the kingdom of heaven. Blessed are they that mourn: for they shall be comforted. Blessed are the meek: for they shall inherit the earth. Blessed are they which do hunger and thirst after righteousness: for they shall be filled. Blessed are the merciful: for they shall obtain mercy. Blessed are the pure in heart; for they shall see God. Blessed are the peacemakers: for they shall be called the children of God. Blessed are they which are persecuted for righteousness' sake: for theirs is the kingdom of heaven. Blessed are ye, when men shall revile you, and persecute you, and shall say all manner of evil against you falsely, for my sake. Rejoice, and be exceeding glad: for great is your reward in heaven: for so persecuted they the prophets which were before you. [*Matt. v.*]

Now therefore hearken unto me, O ye children: for blessed are they that keep my ways. Hear instruction, and be wise, and refuse it not. Blessed is the man that heareth me, watching daily at my gates, waiting at the posts of my doors. For whoso findeth me findeth life, and shall obtain favor of the Lord. But he that sinneth against me wrongeth his own soul: all they that hate me love death. [*Prov. viii.*] Happy is the man that findeth wisdom, and the man that getteth understanding: for the merchandise of it is better than the merchandise of silver, and the gain thereof than fine gold. She is more precious than rubies: and all the things thou canst desire are not to be compared unto her. Length of days is in her right hand; and in her left hand riches and honor. Her ways are ways of pleasantness, and all her paths are peace. She is a tree of life to them that lay hold upon her: and happy is every one that retaineth her. [*Prov. iii.*]

Trust in the Lord with all thine heart; and lean not unto thine own understanding. In all thy ways acknowledge him, and he shall direct thy paths. [*Prov. iii.*] Blessed is the man that trusteth in the Lord, and whose hope the Lord is. For he shall be as a tree planted by the waters, and that spreadeth out her roots by the river, and shall not see when heat cometh, but her leaf shall be green; and shall not be careful in the year of drought, neither shall cease from yielding fruit. [*Jer. xvii.*] Commit thy works unto the Lord, and thy thoughts shall be established. (*Prov. xvi.*)

Lay not up for yourselves treasures upon earth, where moth and rust doth corrupt, and where thieves break through and steal: but lay up for yourselves treasures in heaven, where neither moth nor rust doth corrupt, and where thieves do not break through nor steal: for where your treasure is, there will your heart be also. [*Matt. vi.*]

Love not the world, neither the things that are in the world. If any man love the world, the love of the Father is not in him. For all that is in the world, the lust of the flesh, and the lust of the eyes, and the pride of life, is not of the Father, but is of the world. And the world passeth away, and the lust thereof; but he that doeth the will of God abideth for ever. [*1 John ii.*] Seek ye first the kingdom of God, and his righteousness; and all these things shall be added unto you. Take therefore no thought for the morrow: for the morrow shall take thought for the things of itself. Sufficient unto the day is the evil thereof. [*Matt. vi.*] These things I have spoken unto you, that in me ye might have peace. In the world ye shall have tribulation: but be of good cheer; I have overcome the world. [*John xvi.*]

The hope of the ungodly is like dust that is blown away with the wind; like a thin froth that is driven away with the storm; like as the smoke which is dispersed here and there with a tempest, and passeth away as the remembrance of a guest that tarrieth but a day. But the righteous live for evermore; their reward also is with the Lord, and the care of them is with the Most High. Therefore shall they receive a glorious kingdom, and a beautiful crown from the Lord's hand; for with his right hand shall he cover them, and with his arm shall he protect them. [*Wisdom v.*]

CHILDREN.

At the same time came the disciples unto Jesus, saying, Who is the greatest in the kingdom of heaven? And Jesus called a little child unto him, and set him in the midst of them, and said, Verily I say unto you, except ye be converted, and become as little children, ye shall not enter into the kingdom of heaven. Whosoever therefore shall humble himself as this little child, the same is greatest in the kingdom of heaven. And whoso shall receive one such little child in my name receiveth me. But whoso shall cause one of these little ones which believe in me to stumble, it were better for him that a millstone were hanged about his neck, and that he were drowned in the depth of the sea. Take heed that ye despise not one of these little ones; for I say unto you, that in heaven their angels do always behold the face of my Father which is in heaven. Even so it is not the will of your Father which is in heaven, that one of these little ones should perish. [*Matt. xviii.*] They shall be mine, saith the Lord of hosts, in that day when I make up my jewels; and I will spare them, as a man spareth his own son that serveth him. [*Mal. iii.*]

And they brought young children to him, that he should touch them; and his disciples rebuked those that brought them. But when Jesus saw it, he was much displeased, and said unto them, Suffer the little children to come unto me, and forbid them not; for of such is the kingdom of God. Verily I say unto you, Whosoever shall not receive the kingdom of God as a little child, he shall not enter therein. And he took them up in his arms, put his hands upon them, and blessed them. [*Mark x.*]

A voice was heard in Ramah, lamentation, and bitter weeping; Rachel weeping for her children refused to be comforted for her children, because they were not. Thus saith the Lord; Refrain thy voice from weeping, and thine eyes from tears: for thy work shall be rewarded, saith the Lord. [*Jer. xxxi.*]

When David saw that his servants whispered, David perceived that the child was dead: therefore David said unto his servants, Is the child dead? And they said, He is dead. Then David arose from the earth, and washed, and anointed himself, and changed his apparel, and came into the house of the Lord, and worshipped: then he came to his own house; and when he required, they set bread before him, and he did eat. Then said his servants unto him, What thing is this that thou hast done? thou didst fast and weep for the child, while it was alive; but when the child was dead, thou didst arise and eat bread. And he said, While the child was yet alive, I fasted and wept: for I said, Who can tell whether God will be gracious to me, that the child may live? But now he is dead, wherefore should I fast? can I bring him back again? I shall go to him, but he shall not return to me. [*2 Sam. xii.*]

And it came to pass, when the man of God saw the woman afar off, that he said to his servant: Run now, I pray thee, to meet her, and say unto her, Is it well with thee? is it well with thy husband? is it well with the child? And she answered, It is well. [*2 Kings iv.*]

And David was much moved, and went up to the chamber over the gate, and wept: and as he went, thus he said, O my son Absalom! my son, my son Absalom! would God I had died for thee. O Absalom, my son, my son! [*2 Sam. xviii.*] And the victory that day was turned into mourning unto all the people: for the people heard say that day how the king was grieved for his son. And the people gat them by stealth that day into the city, as people being ashamed steal away when they flee in battle. But the king covered his face, and the king cried with a loud voice, O my son Absalom! O Absalom, my son, my son! [*2 Sam. xix.*]

MEN AND WOMEN.

Though the righteous be prevented with death, yet shall he be in rest. For honorable age is not that which standeth in length of time, nor that is measured by number of years. But wisdom is the gray hair unto men, and an unspotted life is old age. He pleased God, and was beloved of him: so that living among sinners he was translated. He, being made perfect in a short time, fulfilled a long time: for his soul pleased the Lord: therefore hasted he to take him away from among the wicked. This the people saw, and understood it not, neither laid they up this in their minds, that his grace and mercy is with his saints, and that he hath respect unto his chosen. Thus the righteous that is dead shall condemn the ungodly which are living: and youth that is soon perfected the many years and old age of the unrighteous. [*Wisdom iv.*]

Leave thy fatherless children, I will preserve them alive; and let thy widows trust in me. [*Jer. xlix.*] Come, ye children, hearken unto me: I will teach you the fear of the Lord. What man is he that desireth life, and loveth many days, that he may see good? Keep thy tongue from evil, and thy lips from speaking guile. Depart from evil, and do good; seek peace, and pursue it. [*Ps. xxxiv.*] Honor thy father with thy whole heart, and forget not the sorrows of thy mother. Remember that thou wast begotten of them; and how canst thou recompense them the things that they have done for thee? [*Ecclus. vii.*] My son, keep thy father's commandment, and forsake not the law of thy mother: bind them continually upon thine heart, and tie them about thy neck. When thou goest, it shall lead thee; when thou sleepest, it shall keep thee; and when thou awakest, it shall talk with thee. For the commandment is a lamp; and the law is light; and reproofs of instruction are the way of life. [*Prov. vi.*]

Who can find a virtuous woman? for her price is far above rubies. The heart of her husband doth safely trust in her. She will do him good and not evil all the days of her life. She stretcheth out her hand to the poor; yea, she reacheth forth her hands to the needy. Her husband is known in the gates, when he sitteth among the elders of the land. Strength and honor are her clothing; and she shall rejoice in time to come. She openeth her mouth with wisdom; and in her tongue is the law of kindness. She looketh well to the ways of her household, and eateth not the bread of idleness. Her children arise up, and call her blessed; her husband also, and he praiseth her. Many daughters have done virtuously, but thou excellest them all. Favor is deceitful, and beauty is vain: but a woman that feareth the Lord, she shall be praised. Give her of the fruit of her hands; and let her own works praise her in the gates. [*Prov. xxxi.*]

And being in Bethany, in the house of Simon the leper, as he sat at meat, there came a woman having an alabaster box of ointment of spikenard very precious; and she brake the box, and poured it on his head. And there were some that had indignation within themselves, and said, Why was this waste of the ointment made? For it might have been sold for more than three hundred pence, and have been given to the poor. And they murmured against her. And Jesus said, Let her alone; why trouble ye her? she hath wrought a good work on me. For ye have the poor with you always, and whensoever ye will ye may do them good: but me ye have not always. She hath done what she could. Verily I say unto you, Wheresoever this gospel shall be preached throughout the whole world, this also that she hath done shall be spoken of for a memorial of her. [*Mark xiv.*]

Wherefore now, manfully changing this life, I will shew myself such an one as mine age requireth, and leave a notable example to such as be young to die willingly and courageously for the honorable and holy laws. It is manifest unto the Lord, that hath the holy knowledge, that whereas I might have been delivered from death, I now endure sore pains in body, but in soul am well content to suffer these things, because I fear him. And thus this man died, leaving his death for an example of a noble courage, and a memorial of virtue, not only unto young men, but unto all his nation. [*2 Mac. vi.*]

THE AGED.

We spend our years as a tale that is told. The days of our years are threescore years and ten; and if by reason of strength they be fourscore years, yet is their strength labor and sorrow; for it is soon cut off, and we fly away. [*Ps. xc.*] My days are like a shadow that declineth; and I am withered like grass. But thou, O Lord, shalt endure for ever: and thy remembrance unto all generations. [*Ps. cii.*]

If thou hast gathered nothing in thy youth, how canst thou find anything in thine age? O how comely a thing is judgment for gray hairs, and for ancient men to know counsel! O how comely is the wisdom of old men, and understanding and counsel to men of honor! Much experience is the crown of old men, and the fear of God is their glory. [*Ecclus. xxv.*]

The hoary head is a crown of glory, if it be found in the way of righteousness. He that is slow to anger is better than the mighty; and he that ruleth his spirit than he that taketh a city. The lot is cast into the lap; but the whole disposing thereof is of the Lord. [*Prov. xvi.*] Then Abraham gave up the ghost, and died in a good old age, an old man, and full of years; and was gathered to his people. [*Gen. xxv.*] And he died in a good old age, full of days, riches, and honor. [*1 Chro. xxix.*]

O God thou hast taught me from my youth: and hitherto have I declared thy wondrous works. Now also when I am old and grayheaded, O God, forsake me not. Cast me not off in the time of old age; forsake me not when my strength faileth. [*Ps. lxxi.*]

If thou prepare thine heart, and stretch out thine hands toward him; if iniquity be in thine hand, put it far away, and let not wickedness dwell in thy tabernacles. For then shalt thou lift up thy face without spot; yea, thou shalt be steadfast, and shalt not fear: because thou shalt forget thy misery, and remember it as waters that pass away: and thine age shall be clearer than the noonday; thou shalt shine forth, and shalt be as the morning. And thou shalt be secure, because there is hope; yea, thou shalt dig about thee, and thou shalt take thy rest in safety. [*Job xi.*] And thou shalt go to thy fathers in peace; thou shalt be buried in a good old age. [*Gen xv.*] Thou shalt come to thy grave in a full age, like as a shock of corn cometh in his season. [*Job. v.*]

The righteous shall flourish like the palm tree: he shall grow like a cedar in Lebanon. Those that be planted in the house of the Lord shall flourish in the courts of our God. They shall still bring forth fruit in old age; to shew that the Lord is upright: he is my rock, and there is no unrighteousness in him. [*Ps. xcii.*] Hearken unto me, O house of Jacob, and all the remnant of the house of Israel. Even to your old age I am he: and even to hoar hairs will I carry you; I have made, and I will bear; even I will carry, and will deliver you. [*Isa. xlvi.*] Return unto thy rest, O my soul; for the Lord hath dealt bountifully with thee. For thou hast delivered my soul from death, mine eyes from tears, and my feet from falling. [*Ps. cxvi.*]

Remember now thy Creator in the days of thy youth,

while the evil days come not, nor the years draw nigh, when thou shalt say, I have no pleasure in them; while the sun, or the light, or the moon, or the stars, be not darkened, nor the clouds return after the rain: in the day when the keepers of the house shall tremble, and the strong men shall bow themselves, and the grinders cease because they are few, and those that look out of the windows be darkened, and the doors shall be shut in the streets, when the sound of the grinding is low, and one shall rise up at the voice of the bird, and all the daughters of music shall be brought low; also when they shall be afraid of that which is high, and fears shall be in the way, and the almond tree shall flourish, and the grasshopper shall be a burden, and desire shall fail: because man goeth to his long home, and the mourners go about the streets. Or ever the silver cord be loosed, or the golden bowl be broken, or the pitcher be broken at the fountain, or the wheel broken at the cistern. Then shall the dust return to the earth as it was: and the spirit shall return unto God who gave it. [*Eccl. xii.*]

LIFE IMMORTAL.

Thou, O God, art gracious and true, long-suffering, and in mercy ordering all things. For if we sin, we are thine, knowing thy power: but we will not sin, knowing that we are counted thine. For to know thee is perfect righteousness: yea, to know thy power is the root of immortality. [*Wisdom xv.*]

For if ye live after the flesh, ye shall die: but if ye through the Spirit do mortify the deeds of the body, ye shall live. For as many as are led by the Spirit of God, they are the sons of God. For ye have not received the spirit of bondage again to fear; but ye have received the spirit of adoption, whereby we cry, Abba, Father. The Spirit itself beareth witness with our spirit, that we are the children of God: and if children, then heirs; heirs of God, and joint heirs with Christ; if so be that we suffer with him, that we may be also glorified together. For I reckon that the sufferings of this present time are not worthy to be compared with the glory which shall be revealed in us. Because the creation itself also shall be delivered from the bondage of corruption into the glorious liberty of the children of God. For we know that the whole creation groaneth and travaileth in pain together until now. And not only they, but ourselves also, which have the first-fruits of the Spirit, even we ourselves groan within ourselves, waiting for the adoption, to wit, the redemption of our body. For we are saved by hope: but hope that is seen is not hope: for what a man seeth, why doth he yet hope for? But if we hope for that we see not, then do we with patience wait for it. Likewise the spirit also helpeth our infirmities: for we know not what we should pray for as we ought. And we know that all things work together for good to them that love God, to them who are called according to his purpose. What shall we then say to these things? If God be for us, who can be against us? Nay, in all these things we are more than conquerors through him that loved us. For I am persuaded that neither death, nor life, nor angels, nor principalities, nor powers, nor things present, nor things to come, nor height, nor depth, nor any other creature, shall be able to separate us from the love of God, which is in Christ Jesus our Lord. [*Rom. viii.*]

If ye then be risen with Christ, seek those things which are above, where Christ sitteth on the right hand of God. Set your affection on things above, not on things on the earth. For ye are dead, and your life is hid with Christ in God. [*Col. iii.*] Beloved, now are we the sons of God, and it doth not yet appear what we shall be: but we know that when it shall be manifested, we shall be like him; for we shall see him as he is. And every man that hath this hope in him purifieth himself, even as he is pure. [*1 John iii.*]

Let not your heart be troubled: ye believe in God, believe also in me. In my Father's house are many mansions: if it were not so, I would have told you. I go to prepare a place for you. And if I go and prepare a place for you, I will come again, and receive you unto myself; that where I am, there ye may be also. And whither I go ye know, and the way ye know. Thomas saith unto him, Lord, we know not whither thou goest; and how can we know the way? Jesus saith unto him, I am the way, the truth, and the life: no man cometh unto the Father but by me. Peace I leave with you, my peace I give unto you: not as the world giveth, give I unto you. Let not your heart be troubled, neither let it be afraid. [*John xiv.*]

If a man die, shall he live again? all the days of my appointed time will I wait, till my change come. Thou shalt call, and I will answer thee. (*Job. xiv.*)

But some man will say, How are the dead raised up! and with what body do they come? Thou fool, that which thou sowest is not quickened, except it die: and that which thou sowest, thou sowest not that body that shall be, but bare grain, it may chance of wheat, or of some other grain: but God giveth it a body as it hath pleased him, and to every seed his own body. All flesh is not the same flesh: but there is one kind of flesh of men, another flesh of beasts, another of fishes, and another of birds. There are also celestial bodies, and bodies terrestrial: but the glory of the celestial is one, and the glory of the terrestrial is another. There is one glory of the sun, and another glory of the moon, and another glory of the stars; for one star differeth from another star in glory. So also is the resurrection of the dead. It is sown in corruption, it is raised in incorruption: it is sown in dishonor, it is raised in glory: it is sown in weakness, it is raised in power: it is sown a natural body, it is raised a spiritual body. There is a natural body, and there is a spiritual body. Howbeit that was not first which is spiritual, but that which is natural: and afterward that which is spiritual. The first man is of the earth, earthy: the second man is of heaven. As is the earthy, such are they also that are earthy: and as is the heavenly, such are they also that are heavenly. And as we have borne the image of the earthy, we shall also bear the image of the heavenly. Now this I say, brethren, that flesh and blood cannot inherit the kingdom of God; neither doth corruption inherit incorruption. For this corruptible must put on incorruption, and this mortal must put on immortality. So when this corruptible shall have put on incorruption, and this mortal shall have put on immortality, then shall be brought to pass the saying that is written, Death is swallowed up in victory. O death, where is thy sting? O grave, where is thy victory? The sting of death is sin; and the strength of sin is the law. But thanks be to God, which giveth us the victory through our Lord Jesus Christ. Therefore, my beloved brethren, be ye steadfast, unmovable, always abounding in the work of the Lord, forasmuch as ye know that your labor is not in vain in the Lord. [*1 Cor. xv.*)

For we know that, if our earthly house of this tabernacle were dissolved, we have a building of God, a house not made with hands, eternal in the heavens. For in this we groan, earnestly desiring to be clothed upon with our house which is from heaven: if so be that being clothed we shall not be found naked. For we that are in this tabernacle do groan, being burdened: not for that we would be unclothed, but clothed upon, that mortality might be swallowed up of life. [*2 Cor. v.*]

But as touching the resurrection of the dead, have ye not read that which was spoken unto you by God, saying, I am the God of Abraham, and the God of Isaac, and the God of Jacob? God is not the God of the dead, but of the living. [*Matt. xxii.*]

I will bring the blind by a way that they knew not; I will lead them in paths that they have not known: I will make darkness light before them, and crooked things straight. These things will I do unto them, and not forsake them. [*Isa. xlii.*] And it shall be said in that day, Lo, this is our God; we have waited for him, and he will save us. He will swallow up death in victory; and the Lord God will wipe away tears from off all faces; and the rebuke of his people shall he take away from off all the earth: for the Lord hath spoken it. [*Isa. xxv.*]

Now he that hath wrought us for the selfsame thing is God, who also hath given unto us the earnest of the Spirit. Therefore we are always confident, knowing that, whilst we are at home in the body, we are absent from the Lord: (for we walk by faith, not by sight:) we are confident, I say, and willing rather to be absent from the body, and to be present with the Lord. Wherefore we labor, that, whether present or absent, we may be accepted of him. [*2 Cor. v.*]

But as it is written, Eye hath not seen, nor ear heard, neither have entered into the heart of man, the things which God hath prepared for them that love him. But God hath revealed them unto us by his Spirit: for the Spirit searcheth all things, yea, the deep things of God. [*1 Cor. ii.*] For which cause we faint not; but though our outward man perish, yet the inward man is renewed day by day. For our light affliction, which is but for a moment, worketh for us a far more exceeding and eternal weight of glory; while we look not at the things which are seen, but at the things which are not seen: for the things which are seen are temporal; but the things which are not seen are eternal. [*2 Cor. iv.*]

And I saw a new heaven and a new earth: for the

first heaven and the first earth were passed away; and there was no more sea. And I John saw the holy city, new Jerusalem, coming down from God out of heaven. And I heard a great voice out of heaven saying, Behold, the tabernacle of God is with men, and he will dwell with them, and they shall be his people, and God himself shall be with them, and be their God. And God shall wipe away all tears from their eyes; and there shall be no more death, neither sorrow, nor crying, neither shall there be any more pain: for the former things are passed away. And he that sat upon the throne said, Behold, I make all things new. I am Alpha and Omega, the beginning and the end. I will give unto him that is athirst of the fountain of the water of life freely. He that overcometh shall inherit all things; and I will be his God, and he shall be my son. [*Rev. xxi.*] And I heard a voice from heaven saying unto me, Write, Blessed are the dead which die in the Lord from henceforth: yea, saith the Spirit, that they may rest from their labors; and their works do follow them. [*Rev. xiv.*] They shall not hunger nor thirst; neither shall the heat nor sun smite them: for he that hath mercy on them shall lead them, even by the springs of water shall he guide them. [*Isa. xlix.*]

And he shewed me a pure river of water of life, clear as crystal. On either side of the river, was there the tree of life, and the leaves of the tree were for the healing of the nations. And there shall be no night there; and they need no candle, neither light of the sun; for the Lord God giveth them light: and they shall reign for ever and ever. [*Rev. xxii.*] And the city hath no need of the sun, neither of the moon, to shine in it; for the glory of God did lighten it, and the Lamb is the light thereof. And the nations shall walk in the light of it: and the kings of the earth do bring their glory and honor into it. And the gates of it shall not be shut at all by day: for there shall be no night there. [*Rev. xxi.*]

Strengthen ye the weak hands, and confirm the feeble knees. Say to them that are of a fearful heart, Be strong, fear not: behold, your God will come with vengeance, even God with a recompense; he will come and save you. Then the eyes of the blind shall be opened, and the ears of the deaf shall be unstopped. Then shall the lame man leap as a hart, and the tongue of the dumb sing: for in the wilderness shall waters break out, and streams in the desert. And the parched ground shall become a pool, and the thirsty land springs of water. And a highway shall be there, and a way, and it shall be called The way of holiness; the unclean shall not pass over it; but it shall be for those: the wayfaring men, though fools, shall not err therein. And the ransomed of the Lord shall return, and come to Zion with songs and everlasting joy upon their heads: they shall obtain joy and gladness, and sorrow and sighing shall flee away. [*Isa. xxxv.*]

After this I beheld, and, lo, a great multitude, which no man could number, of all nations, and kindreds, and people, and tongues, stood before the throne, and before the Lamb, clothed with white robes, and palms in their hands; and cried with a loud voice, saying, Salvation to our God which sitteth upon the throne, and unto the Lamb. And all the angels stood round about the throne, and worshipped God, saying, Amen: Blessing, and glory, and wisdom, and thanksgiving, and honor, and power, and might, be unto our God for ever and ever. Amen. Who are these which are arrayed in white robes, and whence came they? These are they which came out of great tribulation, and have washed their robes, and made them white in the blood of the Lamb. Therefore are they before the throne of God, and serve him day and night in his temple: and he that sitteth on the throne shall dwell among them. They shall hunger no more, neither thirst any more; neither shall the sun light on them, nor any heat. For the Lamb which is in the midst of the throne shall feed them, and shall lead them unto living fountains of waters: and God shall wipe away all tears from their eyes. [*Rev. vii.*]

Now the God of hope fill you with all joy and peace, that ye may abound in hope, through the power of the Holy Spirit. [*Rom. xv.*]

THOUGHTS OF IMMORTALITY

The soul lives after the body dies. The soul passes through the gate; he makes a way in the darkness to his Father; he has pierced the heart of evil to do the things of his Father.

Then shall the Judge of the dead answer: Let this soul pass on; he is without sin; he lives upon truth. He has made his delight in doing what is good to men, and what is pleasing to God. He has given food to the hungry; drink to the thirsty and clothes to the naked. His lips are pure and his hands are pure. His heart weighs right in the balance. He fought on earth the battle of the good, even as his Father, the Lord of the invisible world had commanded him. O God, the protector of him who has brought his cry unto Thee, make it well with him in the world of spirits! He loved his father, he honored his mother; he loved his brethren. He never preferred the great man to him of low condition. He was a wise man, his soul loved God. He was a brother to the great and a father to the humble; and he never was a mischief-maker. Such as these shall find grace in the eyes of the great God. They shall dwell in the abodes of glory, where the heavenly life is led. The bodies which they have abandoned will repose forever in their tombs, while they will enjoy the presence of the great God. — *Egyptian* (*Book of the Dead*).

Heaven is a palace with many doors, and each one may enter in his own way. There is another, invisible, eternal existence, superior to the visible one, which does not perish when all things perish. Those who attain to this never return. The God of the dead waits enthroned in immortal light to welcome the good into his kingdom of joy; to the homes he has prepared for them, where the One Being dwells beyond the stars. — *Hindu*.

There are treasures laid up in the heart— treasures of charity, piety, temperance, and soberness. These treasures a man takes with him beyond death, when he leaves this world. Man never dies. The soul inhabits the body for a time and leaves it again. The soul is myself; the body is only my dwelling-place. The pearls and gems which a man has collected, even from his youth, cannot go with him to another world. Friends and relations cannot go with him a step further than his place of burial. But a man's actions, good or bad, go with him to the future world. As kindred, friends and dear ones salute him who hath travelled far and returned home safe, so will good deeds welcome him who goes from this world and enters another. — *Buddhist*.

What is death? To be born again an angel of Eternity. — *Persian (Buzurdi)*.

The Supreme Soul, whose work is the universe, always dwelling in the hearts of all being, is revealed by the heart. Those who know him become immortal. — *Hindu*.

The sun rises out of life and sets into life; this is the sacred law; it sways to-day, and will sway to-morrow.

From the unreal, lead me to the real; from darkness to light; from death to immortality! This uttered overcomes the world. — *Hindu (Brihad Upanishad).*

Know that these finite bodies have belonged to an eternal, inexhaustible, indestructible spirit. He who believes that this spirit can kill, and he who believes it can be killed, both are wrong. Unborn, changeless, eternal, it is not slain when the body is slain. * * * * Weapons cannot cleave, nor fire burn it. It is constant, immovable; yet it can pass through all things. * * * * Grieve not then for any creatures, and abandon not thy duty. For a noble man, that infamy were worse than death. * * * * It is good to die doing thy own work. — *Hindu (Bhagavadgitá).*

Virtue is a service man owes himself; and though there were no heaven, nor any God to rule the world, it were not less the binding law of life. It is a man's privilege to know the right and follow it.

Betray and persecute me, brother men! * * * * Earth, hell, heaven, combine your might to crush, — I will still hold fast by this inheritance! My strength is nothing — time can shake and cripple it; my youth is transient — already grief has withered up my days; my heart — alas! it seems well nigh broken now! Anguish may crush it utterly, and life may fail; but even so my soul, that has not tripped, shall triumph, and dying, give the lie to soulless Destiny, that dares to boast itself man's master. — *Hindu (Rámáyana).*

Man must not be carried away by grief, but hasten to

a better mind. Thou hast shed tears: it is enough. * * * * We have given what we ought to grief; now let us do what is becoming. — *Hindu* (*Rámáyana*).

Why lookest thou so dull upon thy friends, thou to whom thy friends were so dear? Thy face seems to smile on us in the bosom of death, as if thou wert alive. We see thy glory still, like sunset on a mountain's head. — *Hindu*.

He who in the morning has seen the right way, may in the evening die without regret. — *Confucius*.

It is right, my friends, that we should consider this: that if the soul is immortal, it requires our care not only for the present time, which we call life, but for all time. He, then, is truly wise, who considers most about his soul; who having adorned his soul, not with a foreign, but with its own proper ornament, — temperance, justice, fortitude, freedom, and truth, — thus waits for his passage to the world of the departed, as one who is ready to go whenever destiny shall summon him.

If death be the journey to another place, and there all the dead are, what good can be greater than this? Be of good cheer about death, and know this of a truth, — that no evil can happen to a good man, either in life or after death. — *Plato*.

The body is a prison, from which the soul must be released before it can arrive at the knowledge of things real and immutable.

The soul of each of us is an immortal spirit, and goes to other immortals to give an account of its actions.

When thou shalt have laid aside thy body, thou shalt

rise, freed from mortality, and become an inhabitant of the kindly skies.

My body must descend to the place ordained, but my soul will not descend: being a thing immortal, it will ascend on high, where it will enter a heavenly abode. Death does not differ at all from life.

Every soul is immortal; for whatever is continually moved is immortal. Every body which is moved from without is soulless, but that which is moved from within, that is, of itself, possesses a soul, since this is the very nature of soul. But if this be the case,—that there is nothing else which moves itself except soul,—soul must necessarily be both uncreate and immortal. — *Plato.*

> All that God works is effortless and calm:
> Seated on loftiest throne,
> Thence, though we know not how,
> He works his perfect will.
> — *Æschylus (The Suppliants).*

> It is shame
> For any man to wish for length of life,
> Who, wrapt in troubles, knows no change for good.
> For what delight brings day still following day,
> Or bringing on, or putting off our death?
> I would not rate that man as worth regard
> Whose fervor glows on vain and empty hopes:
> But either noble life or noble death
> Becomes the gently born. — *Sophocles (Ajax).*

An immortal man established in righteousness is a noble hymn of God. — *Greek.*

Who knows whether to live is not death, and to die, life? — *Euripides.*

I believe Nature, knowing the confusion and shortness of our life, hath industriously concealed the end of it from us, this making for our advantage; for if we were sensible of it beforehand, some would pine away with untimely sorrow, and would die before their death came.

Every one should meditate seriously with himself, that it is not the longest life which is the best, but that which is the most virtuous.

But such exclamations as this, "The young man ought not to be taken off so abruptly in the vigor of his years," are very frivolous, and proceed from a great weakness of mind; for who is it that can say what a thing ought to be?

And who knows but that the Deity, with a fatherly providence and out of tenderness to mankind, foreseeing what would happen, hath taken some purposely out of this life by an untimely death? So we should think that nothing has befallen them which they should have sought to shun,—"For naught that cometh by necessity is hard." — *Plutarch.*

What then do you wish to be doing when you are found by death? I, for my part, would wish to be found doing something which belongs to a man, beneficent, suitable to the general interest, noble. But if I cannot be found doing things so great, I would be found doing at least that which I cannot be hindered from doing, that which is permitted me to do: correcting myself, laboring at tranquillity of mind, rendering to the relations of life their due.

If death surprises me when I am busy about these things, it is enough for me if I can stretch out my hands to God and say: The means which I have received from thee for seeing thy administration of the world, and following it, I have not neglected; I have not dishonored thee by my acts. * * * * That thou hast given me life, I thank thee for what thou hast given: so long as I have used the things which are thine I am content; take them back and place them wherever thou mayest choose; for thine were all things, thou gavest them to me.

I think that what God chooses is better than what I choose; I will attach myself as minister and follower to him. — *Epictetus.*

When I consider the faculties with which the human soul is endowed, * * * * I feel a conscious conviction that this active, comprehensive principle cannot possibly be of a mortal nature. And as this unceasing activity of the soul derives its energy from its own intrinsic and essential powers, without receiving it from any foreign or external impulse, it necessarily follows that its activity must continue forever.

I consider this world as a place which Nature never intended for my permanent abode; and I look on my departure from it, not as being driven from my habitation, but simply as leaving an inn. — *Cicero.*

That which we call death is but a pause or suspension, and in truth a progress to life: only our thoughts look downward upon the body, and not forward upon things to come. It is the care of a wise and good man to look to his manners and actions; and rather how well he lives than how long. To die sooner or later is not the business, but to die well or ill; for death brings us to immortality.

Why was such a one taken away in the prime of his years? Life is to be measured by action, not by time. A man may die old at thirty, and young at fourscore. Nay, the one lives after death; and the other perished before he died. The fear of death is a continual slavery, as the contempt of it is certain liberty. — *Seneca.*

Day and night show unto us the resurrection. The night falleth asleep and the day ariseth; the day departeth and night cometh on. Let us mark how and in what manner the sowing taketh place. The sower casteth into the earth each of the seeds and these decay: then out of their decay the might of the Master's providence raiseth them up and they bear fruit. — *Clement of Rome.*

Vines hold not their clusters all the year; now are they fruitful, and now they shed their leaves like tears. Like the sun, the pure are clouded. On them the envious crowd may hurl its hate; but it is as sparks falling on the clear stream — the sparks perish, the water goes shining on. Fear not the dark, friend; perchance the Water of Life may be found in the dark abyss of sorrow. — *Persian (Saadi).*

> We saw him in the garden, the pleasant garden,
> With his companions and his children, the children he loved.
> His children and his servants blessed him.
> His home was the shelter of happiness.
> > Peace be upon him.
> We saw him giving food to the hungry,
> And clothing to the naked.
> We saw him give help and succor to the aged,
> And good counsel to the young.

> He suffered not the stranger to sleep in the streets:
> He opened his door to the wayfarer.
>   Peace be upon him. — *Syrian Dirge.*

Yes, the very least and the very greatest sorrows that God ever suffers to befall thee, proceed from the depths of his unspeakable love; and such great love were better for thee than the highest and best gifts besides that he has given thee, or ever could give thee, if thou could'st but see it in this light.

God is ever ready, but we are very unready; God is nigh to us, but we are far from him; God is within, we are without; God is at home, we are strangers. The prophet says: "God leadeth the righteous by a narrow path into a broad highway, till they come into a wide and open place": that is, unto the true freedom of that spirit which hath become one spirit with God. God help us all to follow him, that he may bring us unto himself! — *John Tauler.*

Lord, I know not what I ought to ask of thee; thou lovest me better than I can love myself. O my Father, give to thy child that which he knows not how to ask. I dare not pray either for crosses or consolations; I present myself before thee, I open my heart to thee. Behold those wants that I know not myself. See and do according to thy tender mercy.

I adore thy will without knowing it. I am silent before thee; I yield myself up, I would sacrifice myself to thy will, I could have no other desire than to do it. Teach me to pray; pray thyself in me.

O my God! what is death or life to me? Life is nothing; it is even a snare if it be too dear to me.

Death can only destroy this house of clay; it delivers the soul from the contamination of the body, and from its own pride. It frees it from the influence of the tempter, and introduces it forever into the kingdom of truth.

I ask not, then, O my Father, for health or for life. I make an offering to thee of all my days. Thou hast counted them. I would know nothing more. All I ask is to die rather than live as I have lived, and if it be thy will that I depart, let me die in patience and in love. Almighty God, who holdest the keys of the tomb in thy hand, to open and close it at thy will, give me not life if I love it too well. Living or dying, I would be thine. — *Fenelon.*

All death in nature is birth, and in death appears visibly the advancement of life. There is no killing principle in nature, for nature throughout is life; it is not death which kills, but the higher life, which, concealed behind the other, begins to develop itself. Death and birth are but the struggle of life with itself to attain a higher form. —*J. G. Fichte.*

No set words or thoughts will enable us to meet death trustfully. Such trust is God's gift, and the more we detach ourselves from all save Himself, the more "freely He will give us" this, as all other blessings. Once attain to losing self in God, and death will indeed have no sting. —*Jean Nicolas Grou.*

Wherever I may be, through whatever worlds I may be led, I know that I shall forever remain in the hands of the Father who brought me hither, and calls me further on. — *Herder.*

> Then woke
> Stirrings of deep Divinity within,
> And, like the flickerings of a smouldering flame,
> Yearnings of a hereafter. Thou it was,
> When the world's din and passion's voice was still,
> Calling thy wanderer home. — *Williams.*

> What shall I do to gain eternal life?
>   Discharge aright
> The simple dues with which each day is rife,
>   Yea, with thy might.
> Ere perfect scheme of action thou devise,
>   Thy life is fled.
> But he who ever acts as conscience cries,
>   Shall live though dead. — *Schiller.*

He has gone before us. The spirit within him that used to talk to us, to look at us with kind eyes, has left the body, and is no longer visible. Blessings on his memory! May he also, if he behold us, bless us! for we need his blessing. Greatly we need it, with these hopeless yearnings for his presence; these fears that we did not do all we might have done for him; this almost shame at feeling that we are warm and living, while he is cold and motionless; at home and housed, while he is away.

But these are our thoughts, not his. His body is not his spirit; and perhaps his spirit looks upon us this moment, and sees how we loved him, and how we suffer. He knows the struggles that we have still to endure; he looks on his mortal friends with immortal kindness; on these dear relations, on these beloved children. Let us be calm in the hope of rejoining him; let us become patient in it; let us rejoice in it. Let us cherish the thoughts he would desire; let us take up again the duties he would wish us, now and ever, to perform.

O friends that remain! ye will keep as much of me as ye are able; kind thoughts of me; recollections of our mutual joys and sufferings; recollection of the pardon we gave to each other. You will love all whom I have loved, and me in them.

Surely love, and hope, and joy are not confined to us. Surely there are myriads of beings inhabiting the invisible world. Some may have realized their heaven, and are resting. Some may be carrying it further. Some may be helping us, just as we help the bee, or the wounded bird; spirits of dear friends, who still pity our tears, rejoice in our smiles, and whisper into our hearts a belief that they are present.

The heart bids us believe it possible; and oh! whatever good thing the heart bids us believe, let us do our best to believe it; for God has put it there, and its goodness is His warrant for its being cherished. — *Leigh Hunt.*

The immortality of the soul is a truth which is not bright except to the pure in heart.

Through making us hope for immortality, God has made us a promise of it. If faith is the evidence of things not seen, hope is the certainty of them. Hope prophesies to us. Hope makes us free of the universe. I am a pilgrim, and life is what I have to travel over; and oh! I have many dangers and many wants; but hope is my all in all, nearly. Hope is light, and courage, and a staff; and when I sit down, it is a friend to talk with; and when I suffer, it is an angel to stand by and strengthen me ; and when I have wandered away in sin, and repented and returned to the right path, then from hope I get my peace of mind again, and newness of virtue.

The morrow of the world is a purpose in the mind of God, and so is the great to-morrow of my soul. And I can be well contented to have my life subside on the bosom of him in whom the day died away this evening so beautifully, and in whom it will begin again in the morning so grandly.

O, if there is a heaven for our faith, there are friends in it for our love. Love is greater than faith.

There are some great souls, the very thought of whom is an increase of faith.

A truthful heart never breaks; it strengthens to the last. And to the last we will trust. God is almighty; then all things are his mightiness, and all life is his will. * * * * And to us joys shall be the will of God, and so shall pains and sorrows be. Providence is in all things, so that whatever we do not understand shall be to us nothing to be frightened about, but it shall be mystery and the will of God.

I know that darkness is good for me, as well as light, and that it is good for me not to know some things, as well as to know others; and for myself, I can pray to God out of my whole heart, and with the strength of my understanding, "Thy will be done on earth, as it is in heaven"; else there is not a flower, nor an insect, nor a bird, nor an animal, nor a day, nor a man, but might make me question myself to madness.— *William Mountford.*

Know of a truth that only the Time-shadows have

perished, or are perishable; that the real being of whatever was, and whatever is, and whatever will be, *is* even now and forever.

Can the earth, which is but dead, and a vision, resist Spirits, which have reality, and are alive? On the hardest adamant some footprint of us is stamped in. The last rear of the host will read traces of the earliest van. But whence? O Heaven, whither? Sense knows not; faith knows not; only that it is through mystery into mystery, from God to God. — *Thomas Carlyle.*

Of what import this vacant sky, these puffing elements, these insignificant lives, full of selfish loves, and quarrels, and ennui? Every thing is prospective, and man is to live hereafter. That the world is for his education is the only sane solution of the enigma. All the comfort I have found, teaches me to confide that I shall not have less in times and places that I do not yet know. All I have seen teaches me to trust the Creator for all I have not seen. Whatever it be which the great Providence prepares for us, it must be something large and generous, and in the great style of his works.

The love that will be annihilated sooner than be treacherous has already made death impossible, and affirms itself no mortal, but a native of the deeps of absolute and inextinguishable being. — *R. W. Emerson.*

> 'Tis only when they spring to heaven that angels
> Reveal themselves to you; they sit all day
> Beside you; and lie down at night by you,
> Who care not for their presence — muse or sleep —
> And all at once they leave you and you know them!

> Dear Festus, lay me,
> When I shall die, within some narrow grave,
> Not by itself — for that would be too proud —
> But where such graves are thickest: let it look
> Nowise distinguished from the hillocks round,
> So that the peasant at his brother's bed
> May tread upon my own and know it not;
> And we shall all be equal at the last,
> Or classed according to life's natural ranks,
> Fathers, sons, brothers, friends — not rich, nor wise,
> Nor gifted.   In man's self arise
> August anticipations, symbols, types
> Of a dim splendor ever on before,
> In that eternal circle run by life:
> For men begin to pass their nature's bound,
> And find new hopes and cares which fast supplant
> Their proper joys and griefs; and outgrow all
> The narrow creeds of right and wrong, which fade
> Before the unmeasured thirst for good; while peace
> Rises within them ever more and more.
>   If I stoop
> Into a dark, tremendous sea of cloud,
> It is but for a time; I press God's lamp
> Close to my breast — its splendor, soon or late,
> Will pierce the gloom: I shall emerge one day!
>   *Robert Browning.*

The life of the Spirit is the evidence [of immortality]. Heaven begun is the living proof that makes the heaven to come credible. "Christ in you is the hope of glory." It is the eagle eye of faith which penetrates the grave, and sees far into the tranquil things of death. He alone can believe in immortality who feels the resurrection in him already. — *F. W. Robertson.*

> We live in deeds, not years; in thoughts, not breath;
> In feelings, not in figures on a dial.

We should count time by heart-throbs.
　　　　　He most lives
Who thinks most, feels the noblest, acts the best.
Life is but a means unto an end; that end,
Beginning, mean and end to all things, God! — *Bailey.*

We have all felt, when looking above us into the atmosphere, that there was an infinity of space which we could not explore. When I look into man's spirit, and see there the germs of an immortal life, I feel more deeply that an infinity lies hid beyond what I see. In the idea of duty, which springs up in every human heart, I discern a law more sacred and boundless than gravitation, which binds the soul to a more glorious universe than that to which attraction binds the body, and which is to endure though the laws of physical nature pass away. Every moral sentiment, every intellectual action, is to me a hint, a prophetic sign, of a spiritual power to be expanded forever, just as a faint ray from a distant star is significant of unimaginable splendor.

Dream not of a heaven into which you may enter, live as you may. To such as waste the present state, the future will not, cannot bring happiness. There is no concord between them and that world of purity. A human being who has lived without God, and without self-improvement, can no more enjoy heaven than a mouldering body, lifted from the tomb and placed amidst beautiful prospects, can enjoy the light through its decayed eyes, or feel the balmy air which blows away its dust.

Heaven is in truth revealed to us in every pure affection of the human heart, and in every wise and beneficent action that uplifts the soul in adoration and gratitude.

For heaven is only purity, wisdom, benevolence, joy, peace, in their perfected form. Thus the immortal life may be said to surround us perpetually. Some beams of its glory shine upon us in whatever is lovely, heroic, and virtuously happy in ourselves or in others. The pure mind carries heaven within itself, and manifests that heaven to all around.

Immortal happiness is nothing more than the unfolding of our own minds, the full, bright exercise of our best powers; and these powers are never to be unfolded here or hereafter, but through our own free exertion.

The truth is that all action on earth, even the intensest, is but the sport of childhood compared with the energy and activity of that higher life. It must be so. For what principles are so active as intellect, benevolence, the love of truth, the thirst for perfection, sympathy with the suffering, and devotion to God's purposes? and these are the ever-expanding principles of the future life. — *W. E. Channing.*

>So live that when thy summons comes to join
>The innumerable caravan, which moves
>To that mysterious realm where each shall take
>His chamber in the silent halls of death,
>Thou go not like the quarry-slave at night,
>Scourged to his dungeon, but sustained and soothed
>By an unfaltering trust, approach thy grave,
>Like one who wraps the drapery of his couch
>About him and lies down to pleasant dreams.— *W. C. Bryant.*

I see the autumn prefigured in the spring. The flowers of May-day foretold the harvest, its rosy apples, and its yellow ears of corn. As the bud now lying cold and close upon the bark of every tree throughout our northern clime is a silent prophecy of yet another spring and other summers, and harvests too, so this instinctive love of justice, scantily budding here and nipped by adverse fate, silently but clearly tells of the kingdom of heaven.

I cannot think the future world is to be feared, even by the worst of men. I had rather die a sinner than live one. Doubtless justice is there to be done; that may seem stern and severe. But remember, God's justice is not like a man's; it is not vengeance, but mercy; not poison, but medicine. To me it seems tuition more than chastisement. God is not the jailer of the universe, but the Shepherd of the people; not the hangman of mankind, but their Physician; yes, our Father. I cannot fear him as I fear man. I cannot fail to love. * * * * * Does not even the hireling shepherd, when a single lamb has gone astray, leave the ninety and nine safe in their fold, go forth some stormy night and seek the wanderer, rejoicing to bring home the lost one on his shoulders? And shall God forget his child, his frailest or most stubborn child; leave him in endless misery, a prey to insatiate sin, — that grim, bloodthirsty wolf, prowling about the human fold? I tell you no; not God.

The more I live, the more I love this lovely world; feel more its Author in each little thing, in all that is great. But yet I feel my immortality the more. In childhood the consciousness of immortal life buds forth feeble, though full of promise. In the man it unfolds its fragrant petals, his most celestial flower, to mature its seed throughout eternity. — *Theodore Parker.*

> God judges by a light
> Which baffles mortal sight.
> In His vast world above,
> A world of broader love,
> God hath some grand employment for his son. —*Faber*.

More and more do I feel that this nature of mine is the deep ground-warrant for faith in God and immortality. Everywhere in creation there is a proportion between means and ends,— between all natures and their destinies. And can it be that my soul, which, in its few days' unfolding, is already stretching out its hands to God and to eternity, and which has all its being and welfare wrapped up in those sublime verities, is made to strive and sigh for them in vain, to stretch out its hands to — nothing?

"Onward!" is the call of many a great hour of our being; "onward! to the battle — and victory!" And to this earth-strife that presses upon us every day, to this solemn waiting, — to this dim bordering upon the realm of boundless light, is there not a voice that says, "Onward! onward forever!" Beautiful phrase that describes the departed, "they have passed on." Not, "they are dead"; but — "they have passed on"!

Progress, then, is our being's motto and hope. Gaining and losing in this world, rising and falling, enjoying and suffering, are but the incidents of life. Learning, aspiration, progress, is the life of life. Onward! then, pilgrims to eternity! The day is far spent for some of us, the night is at hand; and over its sublime portal through which the evening stars of this world, but the morning stars of eternity, are shining, is written, "Eye hath not seen, nor ear heard, neither have entered into the heart of man, the things which God hath prepared for them that love him."

Death! what art thou to the Christian's assurance? Great hour of answer to life's prayer; great hour that shall break asunder the bond of life's mystery; hour of release from life's burden; hour of reunion with the loved and lost; what mighty hopes hasten to their fulfilment in thee! What longings, what aspirations, breathe in the still night beneath the silent stars; what dread emotions of curiosity; what deep meditations of joy; what hallowed imaginings of never experienced purity and bliss; what possibilities shadowing forth unspeakable realities to the soul, all verge to their consummation in thee! O death! the Christian's death! what art thou but the gate of life, the portal of heaven, the threshold of eternity? — *Orville Dewey.*

> Our birth is but a sleep and a forgetting:
> The soul that riseth with us, our life's star,
>   Hath had elsewhere its setting,
>   And cometh from afar;
>   Not in entire forgetfulness,
>   And not in utter nakedness,
> But trailing clouds of glory do we come
> From God, who is our home. — *Wordsworth.*

Let us learn to look on death as an appointment, not a fatality; as an appointment of our Heavenly Father, who alone has the power; as appointed in wisdom and love, because appointed by him. * * * * * To die, is to be set free; free from the fetters of a body which is dying while it lives, and from the narrow bounds of a restricted state. To die, is to go with our conscience and character only, into the presence of our Judge. To every temple there is a portal, and a passage from the one to the other. This mortal life is the portal which stands before the grand temple of eternity; and death is the passage between them. — *F. W. P. Greenwood.*

The very greatness of that love which makes the hour of separation dark and painful gives rise to high and holy duties in doing the work which we think the purified spirits of our friends would wish to have done. — *Richard Metcalf.*

That future world, instead of a boundless abyss of darkness is a region of life and light. * * * While the sun is above the horizon, the heavens seem empty, and the earth alone seems looked on by that shining orb. But as the sun sinks and the shadows fall across the hills, one by one the stars are ushered into the sky, a glorious host, innumerable worlds, showing forth the wisdom and power of God. Then we perceive how much, all the time, has been around us, and how infinitely more vast and sublime was that which in the brightness of day was unseen, than what was visible. So revelation draws aside from the eye of the spirit the veil between, and we behold the empty void filled with those whom we called dead, alive again. — the mortal become immortal; and the earth itself appears but the threshold of a vast abode, peopled by the creatures and filled with the light of the infinite Love. — *Ephraim Peabody.*

Let us trustingly leave these matters — where, indeed, whether trustingly or not, we must leave them — with the infinite Love which embraces all our loves, and the infinite Wisdom which comprehends all our needs; assured that the Father of the house whose mansions are many, and the Father of spirits whose goal is one, will find the right place and connections and nurture for every soul he has caused to be; that in the eternities the thing desired will arrive at last; that seeking and finding are divinely evened. Let us rest in the thought that life must be richer than all our experience, nay, than our fondest dreams. — *F. H. Hedge.*

When, by nobler culture, by purer experience, by breathing the air of a higher duty, vitality at length creeps into the soul, the instincts of immortality will wake within us. The word of hope will speak to us a language no longer strange. We shall feel like the captive bird carried accidentally to its own land, when hearing for the first time the burst of kindred song from its native woods, it beats instinctively the bar of its cage in yearning for the free air.

A single instant of the Divine life, spread over all that is simultaneous, is worth an eternity of ours, which at least begins by taking all things one by one. And in proportion as we emerge from this childhood of the mind, and claim our approach to union with God, will the contents of our experience enrich themselves, and its area correct its evanescence; till a mere moment may become worth a millennium before; and the Transient may be to the large soul more than the Everlasting to the little : and then whether our Time be long or short by Sun and Moon we may well remain indifferent, since the life that is beyond time and nature is vivid within us.

When, therefore, in higher moments brought by the

sorrows of life, the tensions of duty, or the silence of thought, you catch some faint tones of a voice diviner than your own, know that you are not alone, and who it is that is with you. Stay not in the cold monologue of solitary meditation, but fling yourself into the communion of prayer. Fold not the personal shadows round you; lie open to the gleam that pierces them; confide in it as the brightest of realities, — a path of heavenly light streaking the troubled waters of your being, and leading your eye to the orb that sends it. — *James Martineau.*

The household to which the angel of death has come can never forget his coming. The shadow which his wings have cast over the soul must remain, however clearly the light from God's own love may shine.

Yes, when we are most perfectly resigned to his will, and most perfectly consoled under the loss by the dear promises of Christ, and most happy in the sweet hope of reunion with the dead, and most faithful in using the discipline which we know to be for our own good, the loss, in itself considered, may then seem, as it perhaps then becomes, greater than it ever was before. By the completeness of spiritual experience is the depth of our sorrow revealed. By the spiritual development of our affections the sacredness of earthly affection and of earthly relations is first discerned. A part of the blessing upon those who mourn comes by learning the greatness of their loss.

Hearts which rejoice cannot come so near to each other as hearts which grieve. Tears mingle more perfectly than smiles, and the chain of family love on earth becomes much stronger when some of its links are in heaven.

We need to learn that the purpose of the tree is to bear fruit, not flowers; and that the wisdom and goodness of God may abound only the more at the time when the blossoms fall. — *W. G. Eliot.*

And shall heaven have no children in it? Must none but gray hairs pass through its gates? Or shall not, rather, glad, gleesome children, with flowing hair and merry eyes, go with laughter through its doorways, to meet " their angels " who " do always behold the face of their Father in heaven "?

Let us not forget that there are two sides to dying, — this earth side and the heaven side. The stars that go out when morning comes do not stop shining; only some other eyes in some other land are made glad by them. — *M. J. Savage.*

>   Yet Love will dream, and Faith will trust,
>   (Since He who knows our need is just,)
>   That somehow, somewhere, meet we must.
>   Alas for him who never sees
>   The stars shine through his cypress trees!
>   Who, hopeless, lays his dead away,
>   Nor looks to see the breaking day
>   Across the mournful marbles play!
>   Who hath not learned, in hours of faith,
>   The truth to flesh and sense unknown,
>   That Life is ever Lord of Death,
>   And Love can never lose its own! — *Whittier.*

If this life is all, there is no place for such a faculty as conscience with its lash of remorse in one hand, and its peace like a river, in the other. * * * * * The step from instinct to freedom and conscience, is a step from time to eternity. Conscience is not truly correlated to human life. The ethical implies the eternal.

If I were to construct one all-embracing argument for immortality, and were to put it into one word, it would be — *God.* * * * * It was Christ's realization of the living God that rendered his own conviction of eternal life so absolute.

If the cup of life is full, there is little sense of past or future; the present is enough. * * * * When Christ speaks of eternal life, he does not mean future endless existence; this may be involved, but it is an inference or secondary thought; he means instead fullness or perfection of life. That it will go on forever, is a matter of course, but it is not the important feature of the truth. — *T. T. Munger.*

We talk of immortality; but there is a better phrase than that, — the word of Jesus, " eternal life." That implies not mere duration, but quality. It blends the present and the future in one. It sets before us a state into which we are called to enter now, and into which as we enter we find ourselves at home in our Father's house, beyond the power of doubt and fear.

Mere continuance of existence, — what is it? That bowlder yonder has existed for ages, a very eternity to the imagination; and it is only a bowlder after all. One hour of throbbing human life is worth more than its barren eternity. What is it to you or me whether we go on living, if life to us is made up of petty and ignoble thoughts and occupations? The real trouble with most of us is not the doubt whether we shall live hereafter, but the fact that as yet we have hardly begun to live at all.

Nothing is so completely beyond the power of death as a noble love. Parting can shatter only its outward shell. Under that strange touch, love in its inmost recesses kindles and glows with a divine fire. Whom of the living do we love as we love our dead? Whom else do we hold so sacredly and so surely? Not as a memory of a lost past, — nothing in our present is so real as they, and toward our unknown future we go with a great and solemn gladness, beckoned by their presence. — *Geo. S. Merriam.*

This is the change that comes. We are not afraid any more of our Father. We are not all happy. But if he says go, you will know that it is well, and you will not be afraid. You know it is the Father. Do not say God, that is far off — He is our Father.

And the little Pilgrim's voice echoed away through the great firmament to other worlds. And it breathed over the earth like some one saying Courage! to those whose hearts were failing; and it dropped down into the great confusion and traffic of the land of darkness, and startled many, like the voice of a child calling and calling, and never ceasing, Come! and come! and come! — *Mrs. Oliphant.*

> The leaves, though thick, are falling: one by one
>   Decayed they drop from off their parent tree;
> Their work with Autumn's latest day is done, —
>   Thou see'st them borne upon the breezes free.
> They lie strewn here and there. their many dyes
>   That yesterday so caught thy passing eye;
> Soiled by the rain, each leaf neglected lies,
>   Upon the path where now thou hurriest by.

Yet think thee not their beauteous tints less fair
    Than when they hung so gayly o'er thy head;
But rather find thee eyes, and look thee there
    Where now thy feet so heedless o'er them tread,
And thou shalt see, where wasting now they lie,
    The unseen hues of immortality. —*Jones Very.*

SELECTED POEMS.

PART I.—LIFE AND DEATH.

A Chant.

"*Benedictus qui venit in nomine Domini.*"

Who is the Angel that cometh?
    Life!
Let us not question what he brings,
    Peace or strife;
Under the shade of his mighty wings,
    One by one,
    Are his secrets told;
    One by one,
Lit by the rays of each morning's sun,
  Shall a new flower its petals unfold,
  With the mystery hid in its heart of gold.
We will arise and go forth to greet him,
  Singly, gladly, with one accord,—
    "Blessed is he that cometh
    In the name of the Lord!"

Who is the Angel that cometh?
    Pain!
Let us arise and go forth to greet him;
    Not in vain
Is the summons come for us to meet him;
    He will stay,
    And darken our sun;
    He will stay
A desolate night, a weary day.
  Since in that shadow our work is done,
  And in that shadow our crowns are won,
Let us say still while his bitter chalice
  Slowly into our hearts is poured,—
    "Blessed is he that cometh
    In the name of the Lord!"

Who is the Angel that cometh?
    Death!
But do not shudder and do not fear;
    Hold your breath,
For a kingly presence is drawing near,
    Cold and bright
    Is his flashing steel,
    Cold and bright
The smile that comes like a starry light
  To calm the terror and grief we feel;
He comes to help and to save and to heal:
Then let us, baring our hearts and kneeling,
    Sing, while we wait this Angel's sword,—
      " Blessed is he that cometh
      In the name of the Lord!"

Adelaide Procter.

De Profundis.

The face which, duly as the sun,
Rose up for me with life begun,
To mark all bright hours of the day
With hourly love, is dimmed away,—
  And yet my days go on, go on.

The tongue which, like a stream, could run
Smooth music from the roughest stone,
And every morning with "Good day"
Make each day good, is hushed away,—
  And yet my days go on, go on.

The heart which, like a staff, was one
For mine to lean and rest upon;
The strongest on the longest day
With steadfast love, is caught away,—
  And yet my days go on, go on.

And cold before my summer's done,
And deaf in Nature's general tune,
And fallen too low for special fear,
And here, with hope no longer here,—
  While the tears drop, my days go on.

This Nature, though the snows be down,
Thinks kindly of the bird of June:
The little red hip on the tree
Is ripe for such. What is for me,
    Whose days so winterly go on?

I ask less kindness to be done, —
Only to loose these pilgrim shoon,
(Too early worn and grimed) with sweet,
Cool, deathly touch to these tired feet,
    Till days go out which now go on.

A Voice reproves me thereupon,
More sweet than Nature's when the drone
Of bees is sweetest, and more deep
Than when the rivers overleap
    The shuddering pines, and thunder on.

God's Voice, not Nature's. Night and noon
He sits upon the great white throne
And listens for the creature's praise.
What babble we of days and days?
    The Day-spring he, whose days go on.

He reigns above, he reigns alone;
Systems burn out and leave his throne:
Fair mists of seraphs melt and fall
Around him, changeless amid all, —
    Ancient of days, whose days go on.

For us, — whatever's undergone,
Thou knowest, willest what is done.
Grief may be joy misunderstood;
Only the Good discerns the good.
    I trust thee while my days go on.

Whatever's lost, it first was won:
We will not struggle nor impugn.
Perhaps the cup was broken here
That Heaven's new wine might show more clear.
    I praise thee while my days go on.

I praise thee while my days go on;
I love thee while my days go on;
Through dark and dearth, through fire and frost,
With emptied arms and treasure lost,
I thank thee while my days go on.
Elizabeth Barrett Browning.

Waiting by the Gate.

Beside a massive gateway built up in years gone by,
Upon whose top the clouds in eternal shadow lie,
While streams the evening sunshine on quiet wood and lea,
I stand and calmly wait till the hinges turn for me.

The tree-tops faintly rustle beneath the breeze's flight,
A soft and soothing sound, yet it whispers of the night;
I hear the wood-thrush piping one mellow descant more,
And scent the flowers that blow when the heat of day is o'er.

Behold, the portals open, and o'er the threshold, now,
There steps a weary one with a pale and furrowed brow;
His count of years is full, his allotted task is wrought;
He passes to his rest from a place that needs him not.

In sadness then I ponder how quickly fleets the hour
Of human strength and action, man's courage and his power.
I muse while still the wood-thrush sings down the golden day,
And as I look and listen the sadness wears away.

Again the hinges turn, and a youth, departing, throws
A look of longing backward, and sorrowfully goes;
A blooming maid, unbinding the roses from her hair,
Moves mournfully away from amid the young and fair.

O glory of our race that so suddenly decays!
O crimson flush of morning that darkens as we gaze!
O breath of summer blossoms that on the restless air
Scatters a moment's sweetness, and flies we know not where!

I grieve for life's bright promise, just shown and then withdrawn;
But still the sun shines round me: the evening bird sings on,
And I again am soothed, and, beside the ancient gate,
In the soft evening sunlight, I calmly stand and wait.

Once more the gates are opened; an infant group go out,
The sweet smile quenched forever, and stilled the sprightly shout.
O frail, frail tree of Life, that upon the greensward strows
Its fair young buds unopened, with every wind that blows!

So come from every region, so enter, side by side,
The strong and faint of spirit, the meek and men of pride.
Steps of earth's great and mighty, between those pillars gray,
And prints of little feet, mark the dust along the way.

And some approach the threshold whose looks are blank with fear,
And some whose temples brighten with joy in drawing near,
As if they saw dear faces, and caught the gracious eye
Of him, the Sinless Teacher, who came for us to die.

I mark the joy, the terror; yet these, within my heart,
Can neither wake the dread nor the longing to depart;
And, in the sunshine streaming on quiet wood and .ea,
I calmly stand and wait till the hinges turn for me.
Bryant.

Suspiria.

Take them, O Death! and bear away
    Whatever thou canst call thine own!
Thine image, stamped upon this clay,
    Doth give thee that, but that alone!

Take them, O Grave! and let them lie
    Folded upon thy narrow shelves,
As garments by the soul laid by,
    And precious only to ourselves!

Take them, O great Eternity!
    Our little life is but a gust
That bends the branches of thy tree,
    And trails its blossoms in the dust!
Longfellow.

Dropping Down the River.

Dropping down the troubled river,
  To the tranquil, tranquil shore;
Dropping down the misty river,
Time's willow-shaded river,
  To the spring-embosomed shore;
Where the sweet light shineth ever,
  And the sun goes down no more;
  O wondrous, wondrous shore!

Dropping down the winding river,
  To the wide and welcome sea;
Dropping down the narrow river,
Man's weary, wayward river,
  To the blue and ample sea;
Where no tempest wrecketh ever,
  Where the sky is fair and free;
  O joyous, joyous sea!

Dropping down the noisy river,
  To our peaceful, peaceful home;
Dropping down the turbid river,
Earth's bustling, crowded river,
  To our gentle, gentle home:
Where the rough roar riseth never,
  And the vexings cannot come,
  O loved and longed-for home!

Dropping down the rapid river,
  To the dear and deathless land;
Dropping down the well-known river,
Life's swoln and rushing river
  To the resurrection-land;
Where the living live forever,
  And the dead have joined the band,
  In that fair and blessed land!

Horatius Bonar.

The Deserted House.

Life and Thought have gone away
    Side by side,
  Leaving door and windows wide.
Careless tenants they!

All within is dark as night;
In the windows is no light;
And no murmur at the door,
So frequent on its hinge before.

Close the door, the shutters close,
    Or through the windows we shall see
    The nakedness and vacancy
Of the dark, deserted house.

Come away: no more of mirth
    Is here or merry-making sound.
The house was builded of the earth,
    And shall fall again to ground.

Come away: for Life and Thought
    Here no longer dwell;
    But in a city glorious —
A great and distant city — have bought
    A mansion incorruptible.
Would they could have stayed with us!

Tennyson.

The Charmer.

" We need some charmer, for our hearts are sore
    With longing for the things that may not be;
Faint for the friends that shall return no more;
    Dark with distrust, or wrung with agony.

" What is this life? and what to us is death?
    Whence came we? whither go? and where are those
Who, in a moment stricken from our side,
    Passed to that land of shadow and repose?

"And are they dust? and dust must we become?
  Or are they living in some unknown clime?
Shall we regain them in that far-off home,
  And live anew beyond the waves of time?"

So spake the youth of Athens, weeping round,
  When Socrates lay calmly down to die;
So spake the sage, prophetic of the hour
  When earth's fair morning-star should rise on high.

They found him not, those youths of soul divine,
  Long seeking, wandering, watching on life's shore —
Reasoning, aspiring, yearning for the light,
  Death came and found them — doubting as before.

But years passed on; and lo! the Charmer came —
  Pure, simple, sweet, as comes the silver dew;
And the world knew him not — he walked alone,
  Encircled only by his trusting few.

"Let not your heart be troubled," then he said;
  "My Father's house hath mansions large and fair;
I go before you to prepare your place;
  I will return to take you with me there."

And since that hour the awful foe is charmed,
  And life and death are glorified and fair.
Whither he went we know — the way we know —
  And with firm step press on to meet him there.

H. B. Stowe.

A German Funeral Hymn.

"Here we have no continuing city, but we seek one to come." — HEB. xiii., 14.

Come forth! Come on! with solemn song!
The road is short, the rest is long.
The Lord brought here, he calls away,
  Make no delay,
This home was for a passing day.

Here in an inn a stranger dwelt,
Here joy and grief by turns he felt;
Poor dwelling, now we close thy door,
    The talk is o'er,
The sojourner returns no more.

Now of a lasting home possessed,
He goes to seek a deeper rest.
Good-night! the day was sultry here,
    In toil and fear;
Good-night! the night is cool and clear.

Now open to us, gates of peace!
Here let the pilgrim's journey cease.
Ye quiet slumberers, make room
    In your still home,
For the new stranger who has come.

How many graves around us lie!
How many homes are in the sky!
Yes, for each saint doth Christ prepare
    A place with care;
Thy home is waiting, brother, there.

F. Sachse.

Passing Away.

The fragrance of the rose,
Whose dewy leaves in morning's light unclose,
    Goes not more sweetly up
From its rich heart, as from an incense cup,
  Than thy freed spirit from its earthly shrine
  Passed with the still angel to the rest divine.

Oh no! Thou didst not die!
Thou hast but lain the soul's frail vesture by,
    And soared to that pure height
Where day serene is followed by no night,
  And where the discipline of mortal woe
  No shadow over thee can ever throw.

Death never comes to such
With chillness in the mystery of his touch:
   They gently pass away
As melts the morning star in golden day;
  They leave the places they have known below,
  And through the white gates of the morning go.

   We would not call thee back
To the frail flowers that wither on our track,
   Perhaps to have thy feet
Pierced by the thorns that we so often meet:
  For thou art in that fairer world than ours
  Where love mourns not the fading of the flowers.

   Why should we weep for thee
When thy pure soul from every ill is free?
   Our only tears should flow
For those, the loved, who linger still below,
  From whom the light of thy dear smile is fled,
  Who feel indeed that thou art with the dead.

   We know the gloomy grave
Holds not the spirit which our Father gave;
   That loving, lustrous light,
That made the sphere in which it moved so bright,
  Is shining with a clear and quenchless flame,
  Rekindled at the source from whence it came.

   Thou art not dead! For death
Can only take away the mortal breath;
   And life, commencing here,
Is but the prelude to its full career;
  And Hope and Faith the blest assurance give —
  "We do not live to die! We die to live!"
Anonymous.

Auld Lang Syne.

It singeth low in every heart,
  We hear it, each and all, —
A song of those who answer not,
  However we may call;

They throng the silence of the breast,
    We see them as of yore, —
The kind, the brave, the true, the sweet,
    Who walk with us no more!

'Tis hard to take the burden up,
    When these have laid it down;
They brightened all the joy of life,
    They softened every frown;
But oh, 'tis good to think of them,
    When we are troubled sore!
Thanks be to God that such have been,
    Though they are here no more!

More homelike seems the vast unknown,
    Since they have entered there;
To follow them were not so hard,
    Wherever they may fare;
They cannot be where God is not,
    On any sea or shore;
Whate'er betides, thy love abides,
    Our God, forevermore!

J. W. Chadwick.

The Other Side.

Climbing the mountain's shaggy crest,
    I wondered much what sight would greet
    My eager gaze whene'er my feet
Upon the topmost height should rest.

The other side was all unknown;
    But, as I slowly toiled along,
    Sweeter to me than any song
My dream of visions to be shown.

At length the topmost height was gained;
    The other side was full in view;
    My dreams — not one of them was true,
But better far had I attained.

For far and wide on either hand
   There stretched a valley broad and fair,
   With greenness flashing everywhere, —
A pleasant, smiling, home-like land.

Who knows, I thought, but so 'twill prove
   Upon that mountain-top of death,
   Where we shall draw diviner breath,
And see the long-lost friends we love.

It may not be as we have dreamed,
   Not half so awful, strange, and grand;
   A quiet, peaceful, home-like land,
Better than e'er in vision gleamed.
J. W. Chadwick.

God's-Acre.

I like that ancient Saxon phrase, which calls
   The burial-ground God's-Acre! It is just;
It consecrates each grave within its walls,
   And breathes a benison o'er the sleeping dust.

God's-Acre! Yes, that blessed name imparts
   Comfort to those, who in the grave have sown
The seed that they had garnered in their hearts,
   Their bread of life, alas! no more their own.

Into its furrows shall we all be cast,
   In the sure faith that we shall rise again
At the great harvest, when the archangel's blast
   Shall winnow, like a fan, the chaff and grain.

Then shall the good stand in immortal bloom,
   In the fair gardens of that second birth;
And each bright blossom mingle its perfume
   With that of flowers, which never bloomed on earth.

With thy rude ploughshare, Death, turn up the sod,
   And spread the furrow for the seed we sow;
This is the field and Acre of our God,
   This is the place where human harvests grow!
H. W. Longfellow.

After Death in Arabia.

He who died at Azan sends
This to comfort all his friends:

Faithful friends! it lies, I know,
Pale and white and cold as snow;
And ye say, "Abdallah's dead!"
Weeping at the feet and head.
I can see your falling tears,
I can hear your sighs and prayers;
Yet I smile and whisper this, —
"*I* am not the thing you kiss.
Cease your tears and let it lie:
It *was* mine, it is not I."

"Sweet friends, what the women lave,
For the last sleep of the grave,
Is a hut which I am quitting,
Is a garment no more fitting,
Is a cage from which, at last,
Like a bird my soul hath passed.
Love the inmate, not the room, —
The wearer, not the garb, — the plume
Of the falcon, not the bars
Which kept him from those splendid stars.

"Loving friends! be wise, and dry
Straightway every weeping eye, —
What ye lift upon the bier
Is not worth a wistful tear.
'Tis an empty sea-shell, — one
Out of which the pearl is gone;
The shell is broken, it lies there:
The pearl, the all, the soul, is here.
'Tis an earthen jar, whose lid
Allah sealed, the while it hid
That treasure of his treasury,
A mind that loved him; let it lie!
Let the shard be earth's once more,
Since the gold shines in his store!

"Allah glorious! Allah good!
Now thy world is understood;
Now the long, long wonder ends;
Yet ye weep, my erring friends,
While the man whom ye call dead,
In unspoken bliss, instead,
Lives and loves you, — lost, 'tis true,
By such light as shines for you;
But in the light ye cannot see
Of unfulfilled felicity, —
In a perfect paradise,
And a life that never dies.

"Farewell, friends! Yet not farewell:
Where I am, ye, too, shall dwell.
I am gone before your face
A moment's time, a little space.
When ye come where I have stepped,
Ye will wonder why ye wept;
Ye will know, by wise love taught,
That here is all, and there is naught.
Weep awhile, if ye are fain:
Sunshine still must follow rain;
Only not at death, — for death,
Now I know, is that first breath
Which our souls draw when we enter
Life, which is of all life centre.

"Be ye certain all seems love,
Viewed from Allah's throne above;
Be ye stout of heart, and come
Bravely onward to your home!
La Allah illa Allah! yea!
Thou Love divine! Thou Love alway!"

He that died at Azan gave
This to those who made his grave.

Edwin Arnold.

Our Dead.

Nothing is our own; we hold our pleasures
   Just a little while, ere they are fled:
One by one life robs us of our treaures;
   Nothing is our own except our Dead.

They are ours, and hold in faithful keeping,
   Safe forever, all they took away.
Cruel life can never stir that sleeping,
   Cruel time can never seize that prey.

Justice pales; truth fades; stars fall from heaven;
   Human are the great whom we revere:
No true crown of honor can be given,
   Till we place it on a funeral bier.

How the children leave us: and no traces
   Linger of that smiling angel band;
Gone, forever gone; and in their places
   Weary men and anxious women stand.

Yet we have some little ones, still ours:
   They have kept the baby smile we know,
Which we kissed one day, and hid with flowers,
   On their dead white faces, long ago.

Is Love ours, and do we dream we know it,
   Bound with all our heart-strings, all our own?
Any cold and cruel dawn may show it,
   Shattered, desecrated, overthrown.

Only the dead hearts forsake us never;
   Death's last kiss has been the mystic sign
Consecrating Love our own forever,
   Crowning it eternal and divine.

So when Fate would fain besiege our city,
   Dim our gold, or make our flowers fall,
Death, the Angel, comes in love and pity,
   And, to save our treasures, claims them all.

Adelaide A. Frocter.

The Dead.

The dead are like the stars by day,
    Withdrawn from mortal eye,
Yet holding unperceived their way
    Through the unclouded sky.

By them, through holy hope and love,
    We feel in hours serene,
Connected with a world above,
    Immortal and unseen.

For Death his sacred seal hath set
    On bright and bygone hours;
And they we mourn are with us yet,
    Are more than ever ours; —

Ours by the pledge of love and faith,
    By hopes of heaven on high;
By trust triumphant over death,
    In immortality.

Barton.

Bon Voyage.

There's not an hour but from some sparkling beach
Go joyful men, in fragile ships, to sail
By unknown seas to unknown lands. They hail
The freshening winds with eager hope, and speech
Of wondrous countries which they soon w'll reach.
Left on the shore, we wave our hands, with pale
Wet cheeks, but hearts that are ashamed to quail,
Or own the grief which selfishness would teach.
O Death! the fairest lands beyond thy sea
Lie waiting, and thy barks are swift and staunch
And ready. Why do we reluctant launch?
And when our friends their heritage have claimed
Of thee and entered on it, rich and free,
Oh! why of sorrow are we not ashamed?

H. H.

Here and There.

A little fold of hands,
A little drop of sands,
And the freed spirit stands
   Beyond the veil victorious;
Where the sands of life ne'er run,
And the day is never done,
Eternity is won,
   Eternity all glorious.

Ye, who within life's slow
And long procession go,
Who 'mid the sullen flow
   Of storms and tempests wander, —
Ye name me Death! Ye call
Me cursed for the pall
That once must fold o'er all —
   Birth, they have named me yonder!
Joshua Swan.

Invocation.

Answer me, burning stars of night!
   Where is the spirit gone,
That past the reach of human sight
   As a swift breeze hath flown?
And the stars answered me: "We roll
   In light and power on high;
But, of the never-dying soul,
   Ask that which cannot die."

O many-toned and changeless wind!
   Thou art a wanderer free;
Tell me, if thou its place canst find,
   Far over mount and sea?
And the wind murmured in reply:
   "The blue deep I have crossed,
And met its barks and billows high,
   But not what thou hast lost."

Ye clouds that gorgeously repose
  Around the setting sun,
Answer! have ye a home for those
  Whose earthly race is run?
The bright clouds answered: "We depart,
  We vanish from the sky;
Ask what is deathless in thy heart
  For that which cannot die."

Speak then, thou voice of God within,
  Thou of the deep, low tone!
Answer me, through life's restless din —
  Where is the spirit flown?
And the voice answered: "Be thou still!
  Enough to know is given:
Clouds, winds, and stars their part fulfil —
  Thine is to trust in Heaven."

Mrs. Hemans.

Absence.

What shall I do with all the days and hours
  That must be counted ere I see thy face?
How shall I charm the interval that lowers
  Between this time and that sweet time of grace?

I'll tell thee: for thy sake, I will lay hold
  Of all good aims, and consecrate to thee,
In worthy deeds, each moment that is told
  While thou, beloved one, art far from me.

For thee, I will arouse my thoughts to try
  All heavenward flights, all high and holy strains;
For thy dear sake, I will walk patiently
  Through these long hours, nor call their minutes pains.

I will this weary blank of absence make
  A noble task-time, and will therein strive
To follow excellence, and to o'ertake
  More good than I have won since yet I live.

So may this darksome time build up in me
    A thousand graces which shall thus be thine;
So may my love and longing hallowed be,
    And thy dear thought an influence divine.

Frances Anne Kemble.

The Angel of Death.

Why shouldst thou fear the beautiful angel, Death,
    Who waits thee at the portals of the skies,
Ready to kiss away thy struggling breath,
    Ready with gentle hand to close thine eyes?

How many a tranquil soul has passed away,
    Fled gladly from fierce pain and pleasure's din,
To the eternal splendor of the day;
    And many a troubled heart still calls for him.

Spirits too tender for the battle here
    Have turned from life, its hopes, its fears, its charms;
And children, shuddering at a world so drear,
    Have smiling passed away into his arms.

He whom thou fearest will, to ease its pain,
    Lay his cold hand upon thy aching heart:
Will soothe the terrors of thy troubled brain,
    And bid the shadows of earth's grief depart.

He will give back what neither time, nor might,
    Nor passionate prayer, nor longing hope restore,
(Dear as to long blind eyes recovered sight,)
    He will give back those who are gone before.

Oh, what were life, if life were all? Thine eyes
    Are blinded by their tears, or thou wouldst see
Thy treasures wait thee in the far-off skies,
    And Death, thy friend, will give them all to thee.

A. A. Procter.

The God of the Living.

God of the living, in whose eyes
Unveiled thy whole creation lies!
All souls are thine; we must not say
That those are dead who pass away;
From this our world of flesh set free,
We know them living unto thee.

Released from earthly toil and strife,
With thee is hidden still their life;
Thine are their thoughts, their words, their powers,
All thine, and yet most truly ours;
For well we know, where'er they be,
Our dead are living unto thee.

Not spilt like water on the ground,
Not wrapt in dreamless sleep profound,
Not wandering in unknown despair
Beyond thy voice, thine arm, thy care;
Not left to lie like fallen tree;
Not dead, but living unto thee.

O Breather into man of breath!
O Holder of the keys of death!
O Giver of the life within!
Save us from death, the death of sin,
That body, soul, and spirit be
For ever living unto thee!

John Ellerton.

The Silent Land.

Into the Silent Land!
Ah! who shall lead us thither?
Clouds in the evening sky more darkly gather,
And shattered wrecks lie thicker on the strand.
Who leads us with a gentle hand
Thither, O thither,
Into the Silent Land!

>   Into the Silent Land!
>   To you, ye boundless regions
> Of all perfection! Tender morning visions
> Of beauteous souls! The Future's pledge and band!
>   Who in life's battle firm doth stand,
>   Shall bear Hope's tender blossoms
>   Into the Silent Land!
>
>   O Land! O Land!
>   For all the broken-hearted
> The mildest herald by our fate allotted,
> Beckons, and with inverted torch doth stand
>   To lead us with a gentle hand
>   To the land of the great Departed,
>   Into the Silent Land!
>   *From the German of Salis.*
>   *Longfellow.*

The Future.

> What may we take into the vast Forever?
>   That marble door
> Admits no fruit of all our long endeavor,
>   No fame-wreathed crown we wore,
>   No garnered lore.
>
> What can we bear beyond the unknown portal?
>   No gold, no gains
> Of all our toiling: in the life immortal
>   No hoarded wealth remains,
>   Nor gilds, nor stains.
>
> Naked from out that far abyss behind us
>   We entered here:
> No word came with our coming, to remind us
>   What wondrous world was near,
>   No hope, no fear.
>
> Into the silent, starless night before us,
>   Naked we glide:
> No hand has mapped the constellations o'er us,
>   No comrade at our side,
>   No chart, no guide.

Yet fearless toward the midnight black and hollow,
    Our footsteps fare:
The beckoning of a Father's hand we follow —
    His love alone is there,
    No curse, no care.
E. R. Sill.

From the German of Leopold Schefer

All that God wounds he constantly is healing,
Quietly, gently, softly, but most surely;
He helps the lowliest herb, with wounded stalk,
To rise again.
Deep in the treasure-house of wealthy Nature,
A ready instinct works and moves
To clothe the naked sparrow in the nest,
Or trim the plumage of an aged raven;
Yes, in the slow decaying of a rose,
God works as well as in the unfolding bud;
He works with gentleness unspeakable
In Death itself; a thousand times more careful
Than even the mother by her sick child watching.

The Choir Invisible.

Oh may I join the choir invisible
Of those immortal dead who live again
In minds made better by their presence; live
In pulses stirred to generosity,
In deeds of daring rectitude, in scorn
Of miserable aims that end in self,
In thoughts sublime that pierce the night like stars,
And with their mild persistence urge men's minds
To vaster issues.   So to live is heaven·
To make undying music in the world,
Breathing as beauteous order, that controls
With growing sway the growing life of man.

This is life to come,
Which martyred men have made more glorious
For us who strive to follow. May I reach
That purest heaven; be to other souls
The cup of strength in some great agony;
Enkindle generous ardor; feed pure love;
Beget the smiles that have no cruelty;
Be the sweet presence of a good diffused,
And in diffusion ever more intense.
So shall I join the choir invisible,
Whose music is the gladness of the world.
George Eliot.

Life.

Life! I know not what thou art,
But know that thou and I must part;
And when, or how, or where we met,
I own to me's a secret yet.

Life! we've been long together,
Through pleasant and through cloudy weather;
'Tis hard to part when friends are dear,—
Perhaps 't will cost a sigh, a tear;
Then steal away, give little warning,
    Choose thine own time;
Say not Good Night,— but in some brighter clime
    Bid me Good Morning.
Anna L. Barbauld.

In Memoriam.

Farewell! since nevermore for thee
    The sun comes up our eastern skies,
Less bright henceforth shall sunshine be
    To some fond hearts and saddened eye

There are, who for thy last, long sleep,
    Shall sleep as sweetly nevermore;
Shall weep because thou canst not weep,
    And grieve that all thy griefs are o'er.
R. J.

Prospice.

Fear death? — to feel the fog in my throat,
  The mist in my face,
When the snows begin, and the blasts denote
  I am nearing the place,
The power of the night, the press of the storm,
  The post of the foe;
Where he stands, the Arch Fear, in a visible form,
  Yet the strong man must go:
For the journey is done, and the summit attained,
  And the barriers fall,
Though a battle's to fight ere the guerdon be gained,
  The reward of it all.

. . . .

For sudden the worst turns the best to the brave,
  The black minute's at end,
And the element's rage, the fiend-voices that rave,
  Shall dwindle, shall blend,
Shall change, shall become first a peace out of pain,
  Then a light, then thy breast, —
O thou soul of my soul! I shall clasp thee again,
  And with God be the rest!

Robert Browning.

From the "Threnody."

Wilt thou not ope thy heart to know
What rainbows teach, and sunsets show?
Verdict which accumulates
From lengthening scroll of human fates,
Voice of earth to earth returned,
Prayers of saints that inly burned, —
Saying, *What is excellent,*
As God lives, is permanent;
Hearts are dust, hearts' loves remain;
Hearts' love will meet thee again.
Revere the Maker; fetch thine eye
Up to his style, and manners of the sky.

Not of adamant and gold
Built he heaven stark and cold;
No, ...
Built of tears and sacred flames,
And virtue reaching to its aims;
Built of furtherance and pursuing,
Not of spent deeds, but of doing.
Silent rushes the swift Lord
Through ruined systems still restored,
Broadsowing, bleak and void to bless,
Plants with worlds the wilderness;
Waters with tears of ancient sorrow
Apples of Eden ripe to-morrow.
House and tenant go to ground,
Lost in God, in Godhead found.
R. W. Emerson.

Parting and Welcome.

God giveth quietness at last!
The common way once more is passed
From pleading tears and lingerings fond,
To fuller life and love beyond.

Fold the wrapt soul in your embrace,
Dear ones familiar with the place!
While to the gentle greetings there
We answer here with murmured prayer.

What to shut eyes hath God revealed?
What hear the ears that death hath sealed?
What undreamed beauty, passing show,
Requites the loss of all we know?

O silent land, to which we move,
Enough, if there alone be love!
And mortal need can ne'er outgrow
What it is waiting to bestow!

O pure soul! from that far-off shore
Float some sweet song the waters o'er;
Our faith confirm, our fears dispel,
With the dear voice we loved so well!

J. G. Whittier.

PART II.

RESIGNATION—TRUST.

Ministering Angels.

Brother, the angels say,
  Peace to thy heart!
We, too, O brother, have
  Been as thou art,—
Hope-lifted, doubt-depressed,
  Seeing in part;
Tried, troubled, tempted,
  Sustained, as thou art.

Brother, they softly say,
  Be our thoughts one;
Bend thou with us and pray,
  "Thy will be done!"
Our God is thy God;
  He willeth the best;
Trust him as we trusted;
  Rest as we rest!

Ye, too, they gently say,
  Shall angels be;
Ye, too, O brothers,
  From earth shall be free:
Yet in earth's loved ones
  Ye still shall have part,
Bearing God's strength and love
  To the torn heart.

Thus when the spirit, tried,
 Tempted, and worn,
Finding no earthly aid,
 Heavenward doth turn,
Come these sweet angel-tones,
 Falling like balm,
And on the troubled heart
 Steals a deep calm.

Hymns of the Spirit.

"Not as I Will."

Blindfolded and alone I stand
With unknown thresholds on each hand;
The darkness deepens as I grope,
Afraid to fear, afraid to hope;
Yet this one thing I learn to know
Each day more surely as I go,
That doors are opened, ways are made,
Burdens are lifted, or are laid,
By some great law, unseen and still,
Unfathomed purpose to fulfil,
 "Not as I will."

Blindfolded and alone I wait,
Loss seems too bitter, gain too late;
Too heavy burdens in the load,
And too few helpers on the road;
And joy is weak and grief is strong,
And years and days so long, so long:
Yet this one thing I learn to know
Each day more surely as I go,
That I am glad the good and ill
By changeless law is ordered still,
 "Not as I will."

"Not as I will:" the sound grows sweet
Each time my lips the words repeat;
"Not as I will:" the darkness feels
More safe than light, when this thought steals

Like whispered voice to calm and bless
All unrest and all loneliness;
"Not as I will:" because the one
Who loved us first and best, has gone
Before us on the road, and still
For us will all his love fulfil,
    "Not as we will."

H. H.

Life's Question, and Faith's Answer.

Drifting away like mote on the stream;
To-day's disappointment, yesterday's dream;
Ever resolving — never to mend;
Such is our progress; where is the end?

Whirling away like leaf in the wind;
Points of attachment left daily behind;
Fixed to no principle, fast to no friend;
Such our fidelity; where is the end?

Floating away like cloud on the hill;
Pendulous, tremulous, migrating still;
Where to repose ourselves? whither to tend?
Such our consistency; where is the end?

Crystal the pavement under the stream;
Firm the reality under the dream;
We may not feel it, still we may mend;
How we have conquered not known till the end.

Bright leaves may scatter, sports of the wind;
But stands to the winter the great tree behind;
Frost shall not wither it, storms cannot bend;
Roots firmly clasping the rock at the end.

Calm is the firmament over the cloud;
Clear shine the stars through the rifts of the shroud;
There our repose shall be, thither we tend;
Spite of our waverings approved at the end.

Henry Alford.

Quiet from God.

Quiet from God! how beautiful to keep
    This treasure, the All-merciful hath given;
To feel, when we awake and when we sleep,
    Its incense round us like a breath from heaven!

Who shall make trouble? Not the evil minds
    Which like a shadow o'er creation lower;
The soul which peace hath thus attunèd finds
    How strong within doth reign the Calmer's power.

What shall make trouble? Not the holy thought
    Of the departed; that will be a part
Of those undying things his peace hath wrought
    Into a world of beauty in the heart.

What shall make trouble? Not slow wasting pain,
    Not the impending, certain stroke of death;
These do but wear away, then snap the chain
    Which bound the spirit down to things beneath.

                    Sarah J. Williams.

Restored.

Dust unto dust, the heart makes cry;
Ashes to ashes doth reply.
Shall I see God when I shall die?

My hands are strong, the Lord God says,
My arms are wide, in many ways
My love draws on the better days.

Not in hard earth thou leav'st thine own,
Not in cold ground the life is thrown,
Where I am, none can be alone.

Wherefore, O heart, no longer say
Dust unto dust our own we lay,
Ashes to ashes leave to-day,

But with a faith set heavenward
Say, Life to life we have restored,
Spirit to spirit, God to God.

John Tunis.

Sometime.

Sometime, when all life's lessons have been learned,
   And sun and stars for evermore have set,
The things which our weak judgment here have spurned,
   The things o'er which we grieved with lashes wet,
Will flash before us, out of life's dark night,
   As stars shine most in deeper tints of blue;
And we shall see how all God's plans were right,
   And how what seemed reproof was love most true.

And we shall see how, while we frown and sigh,
   God's plans go on as best for you and me;
How, when we called, he heeded not our cry,
   Because his wisdom to the end could see.
And e'en as prudent parents disallow
   Too much of sweet to craving babyhood,
So God, perhaps, is keeping from us now
   Life's sweetest things, because it seemeth good.

And if, sometimes, commingled with life's wine,
   We find the wormwood, and rebel and shrink,
Be sure a wiser hand than yours or mine
   Pours out this potion for our lips to drink.
And if some friend we love is lying low,
   Where human kisses cannot reach his face,
Oh, do not blame the loving Father so,
   But wear your sorrow with obedient grace!

And you will shortly know that lengthened breath
　　Is not the sweetest gift God sends his friends,
And that, sometimes, the sable pall of death
　　Conceals the fairest boon his love can send.
If we could push ajar the gates of life,
　　And stand within, and all God's workings see,
We could interpret all this doubt and strife,
　　And for each mystery could find a key!

But not to-day. Then be content, poor heart!
　　God's plans, like lilies, pure and white unfold;
We must not tear the close-shut leaves apart,
　　Time will reveal the chalices of gold.
And if, through patient toil, we reach the land
　　Where tired feet, with sandals loosed, may rest,
When we shall clearly know and understand,
　　I think that we will say, "God knew the best!"
　　　　　　　　　　　　　　May Riley Smith.

Yet a Little While.

Oh! for the peace which floweth as a river,
　　Making life's desert places bloom and smile.
Oh! for a faith to grasp heaven's bright forever
　　Amid the shadows of earth's "little while."

A little while for patient vigil-keeping,
　　To face the storm, to wrestle with the strong;
A little while to sow the seed with weeping,
　　Then bind the sheaves, and sing the harvest-song.

A little while midst shadow and illusion,
　　To strive, by faith, love's mysteries to spell;
Then read each dark enigma's bright solution,
　　Then hail sight's verdict, "He doth all things well!"

And he who is himself the Gift and Giver,
　　The future glory and the present smile,
With the bright promise of the glad "forever"
　　Will light the shadows of the "little while."
　　　　　　　　　　　　　　Jane Crewdson.

My Dead.

I cannot think of them as dead,
  Who walk with me no more;
Along the path of life I tread
  They have but gone before.

The Father's house is mansioned fair
  Beyond my vision dim;
All souls are his, and here or there
  Are living unto him.

And still their silent ministry
  Within my heart hath place,
As when on earth they walked with me
  And met me face to face.

Their lives are made forever mine;
  What they to me have been
Hath left henceforth its seal and sign
  Engraven deep within.

Mine are they by an ownership
  Nor time nor death can free;
For God hath given to Love to keep
  Its own eternally.
                            F. L. Hosmer.

The Angel of Patience.

To weary hearts, to mourning homes,
God's meekest Angel gently comes:
No power has he to banish pain,
Or give us back our lost again;
And yet in tenderest love, our dear
And heavenly Father sends him here.

There's quiet in that Angel's glance;
There's rest in his still countenance!
He mocks no grief with idle cheer,
Nor wounds with words the mourner's ear;
But ills and woes he may not cure
He kindly trains us to endure.

Angel of Patience! sent to calm
Our feverish brows with cooling balm;
To lay the storms of hope and fear,
And reconcile life's smile and tear;
The throbs of wounded pride to still,
And make our own our Father's will!

O thou who mournest on thy way,
With longings for the close of day!
He walks with thee, that Angel kind,
And gently whispers, " Be resigned :
Bear up, bear on, the end shall tell
The dear Lord ordereth all things well!"

John G. Whittier.

Under the Cross.

I cannot, cannot say,
Out of my bruised and breaking heart,
Storm-driven along a thorn-set way,
  While blood-drops start
From every pore, as I drag on,
  " Thy will, O God, be done!"

I thought but yesterday,
My will was one with God's dear will;
And that it would be sweet to say,
  Whatever ill
My happy state should smile upon,
  " Thy will, my God, be done!"

Now faint and sore afraid,
Under my cross, heavy and rude,
My idols in the ashes laid,
    Like ashes strewed,
The holy words my pale lips shun,
  "O God, thy will be done!"

Pity my woes, O God!
And touch my will with thy warm breath;
Put in my trembling hand thy rod,
    That quickens death;
That my dead faith may feel thy sun,
  And say, "Thy will be done!"
W. C. Richards.

Auf Wiedersehen.

In Memory of J. T. F.

Until we meet again! That is the meaning
Of the familiar words, that men repeat
    At parting in the street.
Ah yes, till then! but when death intervening
Rends us asunder, with what ceaseless pain
    We wait for the Again!

The friends who leave us do not feel the sorrow
Of parting, as we feel it, who must stay
    Lamenting day by day,
And knowing, when we wake upon the morrow,
We shall not find in its accustomed place
    The one beloved face.

It were a double grief, if the departed,
Being released from earth, should still retain
    A sense of earthly pain:
It were a double grief, if the true-hearted,
Who loved us here, should on the farther shore
    Remember us no more.

Believing, in the midst of our afflictions,
That death is a beginning, not an end,
    We cry to them and send
Farewells, that better might be called predictions,
Being foreshadowings of the future, thrown
    Into the vast Unknown.

Faith overleaps the confines of our reason,
And if by faith, as in old times was said,
    Women received their dead
Raised up to life, then only for a season
Our partings are, nor shall we wait in vain
    Until we meet again!

Henry W. Longfellow.

Forever.

Those we love truly never die,
Though year by year the sad memorial wreath,
A ring and flowers, types of life and death,
    Are laid upon their graves.

For death the pure life saves,
And life all pure is love; and love can reach
From heaven to earth, and nobler lessons teach
    Than those by mortals read.

Well blessed is he who has a dear one dead:
A friend he has whose face will never change —
A dear communion that will not grow strange;
    The anchor of a love is death.

The blessèd sweetness of a loving breath
Will reach our cheek all fresh through weary years.
For her who died long since, ah! waste not tears,
    She's thine unto the end.

John Boyle O'Reilly.

Out of the Depths.

Thou that art strong to comfort, look on me!
  I sit in darkness, and behold no light!
Over my heart the waves of agony
    Have gone and left me faint! Forbear to smite
A bruised and broken reed! Sustain, sustain,
  Divinest Comforter, to thee I fly;
Let me not fly in vain!
  Support me with thy love, or else I die!
Whate'er I had was thine!
  A God of mercy thou hast ever been;
Assist me to resign,
  And if I murmur, count it not for sin!
How rich I was, I dare not — dare not think;
How poor I am, thou knowest, who can see
Into my soul's unfathomed misery;
  Forgive me if I shrink!
Forgive me if I shed these human tears,
That it so hard appears
To yield my will to thine, forgive, forgive!
  Father, it is a bitter cup to drink!

My soul is strengthened! it shall bear
  My lot, whatever it may be;
And from the depths of my despair
  I will look up and trust in thee!

Mary Howitt.

Resting in God.

Since thy Father's arm sustains thee,
    Peaceful be;
When a chastening hand restrains thee,
    It is he.
Know his love in full completeness
Fills the measure of thy weakness;
If he wound thy spirit sore,
    Trust him more.

Without murmur, uncomplaining,
  In his hand
Leave whatever things thou canst not
  Understand.
Though the world thy folly spurneth,
From thy faith in pity turneth,
Peace thy inmost soul shall fill,
  Lying still.

Fearest sometimes that thy Father
  Hath forgot?
When the clouds around thee gather
  Doubt him not.
Always hath the daylight broken, —
Always hath he comfort spoken, —
Better hath he been for years
  Than thy fears.

Therefore, whatsoe'er betideth,
  Night or day, —
Know his love for thee provideth
  Good alway.
Crown of sorrow gladly take,
Grateful wear it for his sake;
Sweetly bending to his will,
  Lying still.

To his own thy Father giveth
  Daily strength;
To each troubled soul that liveth,
  Peace at length.
Weakest lambs have largest share
Of this tender Shepherd's care;
Ask him not, then, " when ? " or " how ? "
  Only bow.

Charles R. Hagenbach.

From "In Memoriam."

LIII.

Oh yet we trust that somehow good
  Will be the final goal of ill,
  To pangs of nature, sins of will,
Defects of doubt, and taints of blood;

That nothing walks with aimless feet;
  That not one life shall be destroyed,
  Or cast as rubbish to the void,
When God hath made the pile complete;

That not a worm is cloven in vain;
  That not a moth with vain desire
  Is shrivelled in a fruitless fire,
Or but subserves another's gain.

Behold, we know not anything;
  I can but trust that good shall fall
  At last — far off — at last, to all,
And every winter change to spring.

So runs my dream: but what am I?
  An infant crying in the night;
  An infant crying for the light;
And with no language but a cry.

LIV.

I falter where I firmly trod,
  And, falling with my weight of cares
  Upon the world's great altar-stairs
That slope through darkness up to God,

I stretch lame hands of faith, and grope,
  And gather dust and chaff, and call
  To what I feel is Lord of all,
And faintly trust the larger hope.

Alfred Tennyson.

There is no Death.

There is no death! The stars go down
  To rise upon some fairer shore;
And bright in Heaven's jewelled crown
  They shine for evermore.

There is no death! The dust we tread
  Shall change beneath the summer showers
To golden grain, or mellow fruit,
  Or rainbow-tinted flowers.

The granite rocks disorganize
  To feed the hungry moss they bear;
The forest leaves drink daily life
  From out the viewless air.

There is no death! An angel form
  Walks o'er the earth with silent tread;
He bears our best loved things away,
  And then we call them "dead."

He leaves our hearts all desolate,
  He plucks our fairest, sweetest flowers;
Transplanted into bliss, they now
  Adorn immortal bowers.

Born unto that undying life,
  They leave us but to come again;
With joy we welcome them — the same,
  Except in sin and pain.

And ever near us, though unseen,
  The dear immortal spirits tread;
For all the boundless universe
  Is life — there are no dead.

E. Bulwer Lytton.

Beyond.

We must not doubt, or fear, or dread, that love for life is only given,
And that the calm and sainted dead will meet estranged and cold in heaven : —
Oh, love were poor and vain indeed, based on so harsh and stern a creed.

Earth's lower things — her pride, her fame, her science, learning, wealth and power —
Slow growths that through long ages came, or fruits of some convulsive hour,
Whose very memory must decay — Heaven is too pure for such as they.

They are complete; their work is done. So let them sleep in dreamless rest.
Love's life is only here begun, nor is, nor can be, fully blest;
It has no room to spread its wings, amid this crowd of meaner things.

Just for the very shadow thrown upon its sweetness here below,
The cross that it must bear alone, and bloody baptism of woe,
Crowned and completed through its pain, we know that it shall rise again.

So if its flame burn pure and bright, here, where our air is dark and dense,
And nothing in this world of night lives with a living so intense ;
When it shall reach its home at length — how bright its light! how strong its strength!

If in my heart I now could fear that, risen again, we should not know
What was our Life of Life when here, — the hearts we loved so much below, —
I would arise this very day, and cast so poor a thing away.

But Love is no such soulless clod: living, perfected it shall rise
Transfigured in the light of God, and giving glory to the skies :
And that which makes this life so sweet shall render Heaven's joy complete.

Adelaide A. Procter.

If Thou Couldst Know.

I think if thou couldst know,
  O soul that will complain,
What lies concealed below
  Our burden and our pain;
How just our anguish brings
Nearer those longed-for things
We seek for now in vain, —
I think thou wouldst rejoice and not complain.

I think if thou couldst see,
  With thy dim mortal sight,
How meanings, dark to thee,
  Are shadows hiding light;
Truth's efforts crossed and vexed,
Life's purpose all perplexed, —
If thou couldst see them right,
I think that they would seem all clear, and wise, and bright.

And yet thou canst not know,
  And yet thou canst not see;
Wisdom and sight are slow
  In poor humanity.
If thou couldst trust, poor soul,
In Him who rules the whole,
Thou wouldst find peace and rest:
Wisdom and sight are well, but Trust is best.
                      Adelaide A. Procter.

Hope's Song.

I hear it singing, singing sweetly,
  Softly in an undertone,
Singing as if God had taught it,
  "It is better farther on!"

Night and day it brings the message,
  Sings it while I sit alone;
Sings so that the heart may hear it,
  "It is better farther on!"

Sits upon the grave and sings it,
  Sings it when the heart would groan,
Sings it when the shadows darken,
  "It is better farther on."

Farther on? Oh! how much farther?
  Count the mile-stones one by one.
No! no counting — only trusting
  "It is better farther on!"

Anonymous.

Prayer for Strength.

Father, before thy footstool kneeling,
  Once more my heart goes up to thee,
For aid, for strength to thee appealing,
  Thou who alone canst succor me.

Hear me! for heart and flesh are failing,
  My spirit yielding in the strife;
And anguish, wild as unavailing,
  Sweeps in a flood across my life.

Help me to stem the tide of sorrow;
  Help me to bear thy chastening rod;
Give me endurance; let me borrow
  Strength from thy promise, O my God!

Not mine the grief which words may lighten;
  Not mine the tears of common woe:
The pang with which my heart-strings tighten,
  Only the All-seeing One may know.

And oh! in my exceeding weakness,
  Make thy strength perfect; thou art strong:
Aid me to do thy will with meekness, —
  Thou, to whom all my powers belong.

Oh! let me feel that thou art near me;
  Close to thy side, I shall not fear:
Hear me, O Strength of Israel, hear me!
  Sustain and aid! in mercy hear!

Anonymous.

No More Sea.

Life of our life, and Light of all our seeing,
  How shall we rest on any hope but thee?
What time our souls, to thee for refuge fleeing,
  Long for the home where there is no more sea?

For still this sea of life, with endless wailing,
  Dashes above our heads its blinding spray,
And vanquished hearts, sick with remorse and failing,
  Moan like the waves at set of autumn day.

And ever round us swells the insatiate ocean
  Of sin and doubt that lures us to our grave;
When its wild billows, with their mad commotion,
  Would sweep us down — then only thou canst save.

And deep and dark the fearful gloom unlighted
  Of that untried and all-surrounding sea,
On whose bleak shore arriving — lone — benighted,
  We fall and lose ourselves at last — in thee.

Yea! in thy life our little lives are ended,
  Into thy depths our trembling spirits fall;
In thee enfolded, gathered, comprehended,
  As holds the sea her waves — thou hold'st us all!
                          Eliza Scudder.

The Eternal Goodness.

Within the maddening maze of things,
  And tossed by storm and flood,
To one fixed stake my spirit clings:
  I know that God is good.

I long for household voices gone,
  For vanished smiles I long;
But God hath led my dear ones on,
  And he can do no wrong.

RESIGNATION — TRUST.

I know not what the future hath
   Of marvel or surprise,
Assured alone that life and death
   His mercy underlies.

And if my heart and flesh are weak
   To bear an untried pain,
The bruised reed he will not break,
   But strengthen and sustain.

And so beside the silent sea
   I wait the muffled oar;
No harm from him can come to me
   On ocean or on shore.

I know not where his islands lift
   Their fronded palms in air;
I only know I cannot drift
   Beyond his love and care.
                John G. Whittier.

Blessed are They that Mourn.

Oh, deem not they are blessed alone
   Whose lives a peaceful tenor keep!
The Power who pities man, hath shown
   A blessing for the eyes that weep.

The light of smiles shall fill again
   The lids that overflow with tears;
And weary hours of woe and pain
   Are promises of happier years.

There is a day of sunny rest
   For every dark and troubled night;
And grief may bide an evening guest,
   But joy shall come with early light.

And thou who, o'er thy friend's low bier,
    Dost shed the bitter drops like rain,
Hope that a brighter, happier sphere
    Will give him to thy arms again.

Nor let the good man's trust depart,
    Though life its common gifts deny, —
Though with a pierced and bleeding heart,
    And spurned of men, he goes to die.

For God hath marked each sorrowing day
    And numbered every secret tear,
And heaven's long age of bliss shall pay
    For all his children suffer here.

William C. Bryant.

Faith.

I will not think the last farewell we hear,
    Is more than brief "good-bye" that a friend saith,
Turning toward home, that to our home lies near;
    I will not think so harshly of kind death.

I will not think the last looks of dear eyes,
    Fade with the light that fades of our dim air;
But that the apparent glories of the skies
    Weigh down their lids with beams too bright to bear.

Our dead have left us for no dark, strange lands,
    Unwelcomed there, and with no friends to meet;
But hands of angels hold the trembling hands,
    And hands of angels guide the faltering feet.

I will not think the soul gropes dumb and blind,
    A brief space through our world, death-doomed from birth;
I will not think that Love shall ever find
    A fairer heaven than he made of earth.

Pakenham Beatty.

Good-Bye, till Morning.

"Good-bye, till morning come again!"
We part, but not with aught of pain,
The night is short, and hope is sweet,
It fills our hearts and wings our feet;
  And so we sing the glad refrain,
  "Good-bye, till morning come again!"

"Good-bye, till morning come again!"
The shade of death brings thought of pain,
But could we know how short the night
That falls and hides them from our sight,
  Our hearts would sing the glad refrain,
  "Good-bye, till morning come again!"
M. G. T.

From "The Excursion."

    One adequate support
For the calamities of mortal life
Exists, one only;—an assured belief
That the procession of our fate, howe'er
Sad or disturbed, is ordered by a Being
Of infinite benevolence and power,
Whose everlasting purposes embrace
All accidents, converting them to Good.

    The darts of anguish fix not where the seat
Of suffering hath been thoroughly fortified
By acquiescence in the Will Supreme
For time and for eternity; by faith,
Faith absolute in God, including hope;
And the defence that lies in boundless love
Of his perfections; with habitual dread
Of aught unworthily conceived, endured
Impatiently, ill done or left undone,
To the dishonor of his holy Name.
Soul of souls, and safeguard of the world,
Sustain, thou only canst, the sick of heart!
William Wordsworth.

Venturi Salutamus.

Our beloved have departed,
While we tarry, heavy-hearted,
 In the dreary, empty house:
They have ended life's brief story,
They have reached the home of glory,
 Over death victorious.

Hush that sobbing, weep more lightly;
On we travel, daily, nightly,
 To the rest that they have found.
Are we not upon the river,
Sailing fast, to meet forever
 On more holy, happy ground?

On we haste, to home invited,
There with friends to be united
 In a surer bond than here;
Meeting soon, and met forever!
Glorious Hope, forsake us never,
 For thy glimmering light is dear!

Ah! the way is shining clearer,
As we journey ever nearer
 To the everlasting home;
Comrades, who await our landing,
Friends, who round the throne are standing,
 We salute you, and we come!
  From the German.
   (*Littell's "Living Age."*)

From "My Psalm."

All as God wills, who wisely heeds
 To give or to withhold,
And knoweth more of all my needs
 Than all my prayers have told!

Enough that blessings undeserved
    Have marked my erring track; —
That wheresoe'er my feet have swerved,
    His chastening turned me back; —

That more and more a Providence
    Of love is understood,
Making the springs of time and sense
    Sweet with eternal good; —

That death seems but a covered way
    Which opens into light,
Wherein no blinded child can stray
    Beyond the Father's sight; —

That care and trial seem at last,
    Through Memory's sunset air,
Like mountain ranges overpast,
    In purple distance fair; —

That all the jarring notes of life
    Seem blending in a psalm,
And all the angles of its strife
    Slow rounding into calm.

And so the shadows fall apart,
    And so the west winds play;
And all the windows of my heart
    I open to the day.

J. G. Whittier.

Death of a Sister.

I will not mock thee with the poor world's common
    And heartless phrase,
Nor wrong the memory of a sainted woman
    With idle praise.

With silence only as their benediction,
    God's angels come
Where, in the shadow of a great affliction,
    The soul sits dumb!

Yet would I say what thy own heart approveth;
  Our Father's will,
Calling to him the dear one whom he loveth,
  Is mercy still.

God calls our loved ones, but we lose not wholly
  What he hath given;
They live on earth, in thought and deed, as truly
  As in his heaven.

Up, then, my brother! Lo, the fields of harvest
  Lie white in view!
She lives and loves thee, and the God thou servest
  To both is true.

J. G. Whittier.

PART III.

A GOOD LIFE.

From the "Elegy on the Death of Dr. Channing."

I do not come to weep above thy pall,
    And mourn the dying out of noble powers;
The poet's clearer eye should see, in all
    Earth's seeming woe, the seed of Heaven's flowers.

Truth needs no champions: in the infinite deep
    Of everlasting Soul her strength abides;
From Nature's heart her mighty pulses leap,
    Through Nature's veins her strength, undying, tides.

Peace is more strong than war, and gentleness,
    Where force were vain, makes conquest o'er the wave;
And love lives on and hath a power to bless,
    When they who loved are hidden in the grave.

No power can die that ever wrought for Truth;
    Thereby a law of Nature it became,
And lives unwithered in its sinewy youth,
    When he who called it forth is but a name.

Therefore I cannot think thee wholly gone;
    The better part of thee is with us still;
The soul its hampering clay aside hath thrown,
    And only freer wrestles with the Ill.

Thou livest in the life of all good things;
    What words thou spak'st for Freedom shall not die;
Thou sleepest not, for now thy Love hath wings
    To soar where hence thy Hope could hardly fly.

And often, from that other world, on this
  Some gleams from great souls gone before may shine,
To shed on struggling hearts a clearer bliss,
  And clothe the Right with lustre more divine.

Thou art not idle: in thy higher sphere
  Thy spirit bends itself to loving tasks,
And strength to perfect what it dreamed of here
  Is all the crown and glory that it asks.

For sure, in Heaven's wide chambers, there is room
  For love and pity, and for helpful deeds;
Else were our summons thither but a doom
  To life more vain than this in clayey weeds.

Farewell! good man, good angel now! this hand
  Soon, like thine own, shall lose its cunning too;
Soon shall this soul, like thine, bewildered stand,
  Then leap to thread the free, unfathomed blue.

This laurel-leaf I cast upon thy bier;
  Let worthier hands than these thy wreath entwine;
Upon thy hearse I shed no useless tear, —
  For us weep rather thou in calm divine!

J. R. Lowell.

Well Done.

Servant of God, well done! They serve God well,
Who serve his creatures; when the funeral bell
Tolls for the dead, there's nothing left of all
That decks the scutcheon and the velvet pall
Save this. The coronet is empty show:
The strength and loveliness are hid below:
The shifting wealth to others hath accrued:
And learning cheers not the grave's solitude:
What's done, is what remains! Ah, blessed they
Who leave completed tasks of love to stay
And answer mutely for them, being dead:
Life was not purposeless, though Life be fled.

Caroline Norton.
The Lady of La Garaye.

In Memoriam.

F. D. B.

To pass through life beloved as few are loved,
To prove the joys of earth as few have proved,
And still to keep thy soul's white robe unstained,
Such is the victory which thou hast gained.

How few like thine, the pilgrim feet have come
Unworn, unwounded, to the heavenly home!
Yet He who guides in sorrow's sorest need,
As well by pleasant paths his own may lead.

And love, that guides where wintry tempests beat,
To thee was shelter from the summer heat.
What need for grief to blight, or ills annoy,
The heart whose God was her exceeding joy?

And so that radiant path, all sweet and pure,
Found fitting close in perfect peace secure;
No haste to go, no anxious wish to stay,
No childish terror of the untried way.

But wrapped in trance of holy thought and prayer,
Yet full of human tenderness and care,
Undimmed its lustre and unchilled its love,
Thy spirit passed to cloudless light above.

In the far North, where, over frosts and gloom,
The midnight skies with rosy brightness bloom,
There comes in all the year one day complete,
Wherein the sunset and the sunrise meet.

So, in the region of thy fearless faith,
No hour of darkness marked the approach of death;
But, ere the evening splendor was withdrawn,
Fair flashed the light along the hills of dawn.

Eliza Scudder.

The Friend's Burial.

Her still and quiet life flowed on
  As meadow streamlets flow,
Where fresher green reveals alone
  The noiseless ways they go.

Her path shall brighten more and more
  Unto the perfect day;
She cannot fail of peace who bore
  Such peace with her away.

O sweet, calm face, that seemed to wear
  The look of sins forgiven!
O voice of prayer, that seemed to bear
  Our own needs up to heaven!

How reverent in our midst she stood,
  Or knelt in grateful praise!
What grace of Christian womanhood
  Was in her household ways!

For still her holy living meant
  No duty left undone;
The heavenly and the human blent
  Their kindred loves in one.

She kept her line of rectitude
  With love's unconscious ease:
Her kindly instincts understood
  All gentle courtesies.

The dear Lord's best interpreters
  Are humble human souls;
The Gospel of a life like hers
  Is more than books or scrolls.

From scheme and creed the light goes out,
  The saintly fact survives;
The blessed Master none can doubt
  Revealed in holy lives.

J. G. Whittier.

To J. S.

God gives us love. Something to love
    He lends us; but, when love is grown
To ripeness, that on which it throve
    Falls off, and love is left alone.

And though mine own eyes fill with dew,
    Drawn from the spirit through the brain,
I will not even preach to you,
    " Weep, weeping dulls the inward pain."

I will not say " God's ordinance
    Of death is blown in every wind;"
For that is not a common chance
    That takes away a noble mind.

Sleep sweetly, tender heart, in peace;
    Sleep, holy spirit, blessed soul,
While the stars burn, the moons increase,
    And the great ages onward roll.

Sleep till the end, true soul and sweet,
    Nothing comes to thee new or strange;
Sleep full of rest from head to feet;
    Lie still, dry dust, secure of change.

                      Alfred Tennyson.

G. L. S.

He has done the work of a true man, —
    Crown him, honor him, love him.
Weep over him, tears of woman,
    Stoop, manliest brows, above him!

For the warmest of hearts is frozen,
    The freest of hands is still;
And the gap in our picked and chosen
    The long years may not fill.

No duty could overtask him,
  No need his will outrun;
Or ever our lips could ask him,
  His hands the work had done.

He forgot his own soul for others,
  Himself to his neighbor lending;
He found the Lord in his suffering brothers,
  And not in the clouds descending.

Ah, well! — The world is discreet;
  There are plenty to pause and wait;
But here was a man who set his feet
  Sometimes in advance of fate.

Never rode to the wrong's redressing
  A worthier paladin;
Shall he not hear the blessing,
  "Good and faithful, enter in!"

J. G. Whittier.

A Memorial.

Oh, thicker, deeper, darker growing,
  The solemn vista to the tomb
Must know henceforth another shadow,
  And give another cypress room.

To homely joys and loves and friendships
  Thy genial nature fondly clung;
And so the shadow on the dial
  Ran back and left thee always young.

And who could blame the generous weakness,
  Which, only to thyself unjust,
So overprized the worth of others,
  And dwarfed thy own with self-distrust?

All hearts grew warmer in the presence
  Of one who, seeking not his own,
Gave freely for the love of giving,
  Nor reaped for self the harvest sown.

A GOOD LIFE.

Thy greeting smile was pledge and prelude
    Of generous deeds and kindly words;
In thy large heart were fair guest-chambers,
    Open to sunrise and the birds!

The task was thine to mould and fashion
    Life's plastic newness into grace;
To make the boyish heart heroic,
    And light with thought the maiden's face.

O'er all the land in town and prairie,
    With bended heads of mourning, stand
The living forms that owe their beauty
    And fitness to thy shaping hand.

O friend! if thought and sense avail not
    To know thee henceforth as thou art,
That all is well with thee forever
    I trust the instincts of my heart.

Thine be the quiet habitations,
    Thine the green pastures, blossom-sown,
And smiles of saintly recognition
    As sweet and tender as thy own.

Thou com'st not from the hush and shadow
    To meet us, but to thee we come;
With thee we never can be strangers,
    And where thou art must still be home.

J. G. Whittier.

E. S. G.

"At eve there shall be light," the promise runs
    In the dear volume that he loved so well;
Ay, and for him the promise was fulfilled,
    When rang for him the solemn vesper-bell.

His was no day of sweet, unsullied blue,
    And bright, warm sunshine on the grass and flowers;
But many a cloud of loss and grief and pain
    Dropped its deep shadow on the fleeting hours.

For still, though hours were his, serene and still,
  And radiant hours of steady glowing noon,
That cloud of pain was ever near to touch
  With quivering sadness every brightest boon.

And, as his afternoon drew on to eve
  And still he lingered in the whitened field,
The reapers were so few, till night should fall
  Fain would his hand the heavy sickle wield, —

Darker it grew and darker o'er the land,
  And he was forced to lay the sickle by;
But did it brighten, then his hand was quick
  To seize once more its opportunity.

So the day faded, and the evening came;
  Then from the sky the clouds were furled away,
And a great peace and beauty welcomed in
  The evening star with her benignant ray.

And all the air was hushed and whispering,
  And all the sky was purely, softly bright;
And so the blessed promise was fulfilled;
  "At eve," it said, — "at eve there shall be light."

But that fair evening did not end in night,
  With shadows deep, and darkness all forlorn,
Just at its brightest he was snatched away
  Into the golden palaces of morn.

And surely since the Master went that way,
  To welcome there earth's holiest and best,
He has not welcomed one who loved him more
  Than he who leaned that evening on his breast.

J. W. Chadwick.

In Memory of the Lady Augusta Stanley.

O blessed life of service and of love!
  Heart wide as life, deep as life's deepest woe;
God's servants serve him day and night above,
  Thou servedst day and night, we thought, below.

Hands full of blessings, lavished far and wide,
  Hands tender to bind up hearts wounded sore;
Stooping quite down earth's lowest needs beside, —
  Master, like thee! we thought, and said no more.

We o'er all sorrow would have raised thee up,
  Crowned with life's choicest blossoms night and morn;
God made thee drink of his beloved's cup,
  And crowned thee with the Master's crown of thorn.

Looking from thee to him, once wounded sore,
  We learned a little more his face to see;
Then looking from the cross for us he bore,
  To thine, we almost understood for thee!

Till now, again! we gaze on thee above,
  Strong and unwearied, serving day and night;
O blessed life of service and of love!
  Master, like thee, and with thee in thy light!

Elizabeth Charles.

Charles Lowe.

"If ye love me," Jesus said,
Just before his spirit sped,
"Ye would all rejoice, for know
To my Father I shall go."

As we loved our brother here,
We will check the starting tear,
And rejoice that soul new-born
To his Father now has gone.

Thanks to God for life so pure,
Strong to do, to bear, endure;
Thanks for faith that feared no cross,
Thanks for hope that knew no loss.

Thanks for love so deep and strong,
Love of right and hate of wrong;
Love, unwelcome truth could tell
Just because it loved so well.

Love embracing in its span
Truth and right, and God and man;
Love so loyal and so sweet
It could every duty meet.

Love that cast out every fear,
As the parting hour drew near;
Love that clasped the Father's hand,
Leading to the brighter land.

Risen brother! from above
Let us all still feel thy love;
Earth was fairer for thy stay,
Heaven is nearer us to-day.

W. P. Tilden.

From "Rugby Chapel."

O strong soul, by what shore
Tarriest thou now? For that force,
Surely, has not been left vain!
Somewhere, surely, afar,
In the sounding labor-house vast
Of being is practised that strength,
Zealous, beneficent, firm!

Yes, in some far-shining sphere,
Conscious or not of the past,
Still thou performest the word
Of the Spirit in whom thou dost live —
Prompt, unwearied, as here!
Still thou upraisest with zeal
The humble good from the ground,
Sternly repressest the bad!
Still, like a trumpet, dost rouse
Those who with half-open eyes
Tread the border-land dim
'Twixt vice and virtue; reviv'st,
Succourest! — this was thy work,
This was thy life upon earth.

A GOOD LIFE.

Servants of God! — or sons
Shall I not call you? because
Not as servants ye knew
Your Father's innermost mind,
His, who unwillingly sees
One of his little ones lost —
Yours is the praise, if mankind
Hath not as yet in its march
Fainted, and fallen, and died!

See! In the rocks of the world
Marches the host of mankind,
A feeble, wavering line.
Where are they tending? — A God
Marshalled them, gave them their goal. —
Ah, but the way is so long!
Then, in such hour of need
Of your fainting, dispirited race,
Ye, like angels appear,
Radiant with ardor divine.
Beacons of hope, ye appear!
Languor is not in your heart,
Weakness is not in your word,
Weariness not on your brow.
Ye alight in our van! at your voice,
Panic, despair, flee away.
Ye move through the ranks, recall
The stragglers, refresh the outworn,
Praise, re-inspire the brave.
Order, courage, return;
Eyes rekindling, and prayers,
Follow your steps as ye go.
Ye fill up the gaps in our files,
Strengthen the wavering line,
Stablish, continue our march,
On, to the bound of the waste,
On, to the City of God.

Matthew Arnold.

PART IV.

SUFFERING AND REST.

The Sleep.

"He giveth His beloved sleep." Ps. cxxvii: 2.

Of all the thoughts of God that are
Borne inward unto souls afar,
Along the Psalmist's music deep,
   Now tell me if that any is,
   For gift or grace, surpassing this —
"He giveth his beloved, sleep"?

What would we give to our beloved?
The hero's heart to be unmoved,
The poet's star-tuned harp to sweep,
   The patriot's voice to teach and rouse,
   The monarch's crown to light the brows?
"He giveth his beloved, sleep."

What do we give to our beloved?
A little faith all undisproved,
A little dust to overweep,
   And bitter memories to make
   The whole earth blasted for our sake.
"He giveth his beloved, sleep."

"Sleep soft, beloved!" we sometimes say,
But have no tune to charm away
Sad dreams that through the eyelids creep;
   But never doleful dream again
   Shall break the happy slumber, when
"He giveth his beloved, sleep."

O earth, so full of dreary noises!
O men, with wailing in your voices!
O delvëd gold, the wailers heap!
   O strife, O curse, that o'er it fall!
   God strikes a silence through you all,
  And "giveth his beloved, sleep."

His dews drop mutely on the hill,
His cloud above it saileth still,
Though on its slope men sow and reap.
   More softly than the dew is shed,
   Or cloud is floated overhead,
  "He giveth his beloved, sleep."

For me, my heart that erst did go
Most like a tired child at a show,
That sees through tears the mummers leap,
   Would now its wearied vision close,
   Would childlike on his love repose,
  Who "giveth his beloved, sleep!"

And friends, dear friends, — when it shall be
That this low breath is gone from me,
And round my bier ye come to weep,
   Let one, most loving of you all,
   Say, "Not a tear must o'er her fall —
  "He giveth his beloved, sleep."
                     E. B. Browning.

Epitaph on an Old Maid.

Rest, gentle traveller, on life's toilsome way;
Pause here awhile; yet o'er this lifeless clay
No weeping, but a joyful tribute pay.

No chosen spot of earth she called her own;
She reaped no harvest in her spring-time sown;
Yet always in her path some flowers were strown.

No dear ones were her own peculiar care,
So was her bounty free as heaven's air;
For every claim she had enough to spare.

And loving more the heart to give than lend,
Though oft deceived in many a trusty friend,
She hoped, believed and trusted to the end.

She had her joys: 'twas joy to live, to love,
To labor in the world with God above,
And tender hearts that ever near did move.

She had her griefs: but why recount them here, —
The heartsick loneliness, the onlooking fear,
The days of desolation, dark and drear,

Since every agony left peace behind,
And healing came on every stormy wind,
And with pure brightness every cloud was lined.

And every loss sublimed some low desire,
And every sorrow helped her to aspire,
Till waiting angels bade her go up higher!

Anonymous.

In Harbor.

I think it is over, over —
  I think it is over at last:
Voices of foeman and lover,
  The sweet and the bitter have passed:
Life, like a tempest of ocean,
  Hath outblown its ultimate blast.
    There's but a faint sobbing seaward,
    While the calm of the tide deepens leeward,
    And behold! like the welcoming quiver
    Of heart-pulses throbbed through the river,
    Those lights in the Harbor at last —
    The heavenly Harbor at last!

I feel it is over, over —
  The winds and the waters surcease:
How few were the days of the Rover
  That smiled in the beauty of peace!
And distant and dim was the omen
  That hinted redress or release.
      From the ravage of Life and its riot,
      What marvel I yearn for the quiet
      Which bides in the Harbor at last? —
      For the lights with their welcoming quiver
      That throb through the sanctified river,
      Which girdles the Harbor at last —
      The heavenly Harbor at last?

I know it is over, over —
  I know it is over at last:
Down sail; the sheathed anchor uncover,
  For the stress of the voyage has passed:
Life, like a tempest of ocean,
  Hath outblown its ultimate blast.
      There's but a faint sobbing seaward,
      While the calm of the tide deepens leeward,
      And behold! like the welcoming quiver
      Of heart-pulses throbbed through the river,
      Those lights in the Harbor at last!
      The heavenly Harbor at last!
            Paul H. Hayne.

Out of the Shadow.

Gentle friends who gather here,
With no gloom surround this bier,
Drop no unavailing tear.

Bid this weary frame oppressed
Welcome to its longed-for rest
On the fair earth's sheltering breast.

And the spirit, freed from clay,
Give glad leave to soar away,
Singing, to the eternal day.

When this sentient life began,
Love of nature, love of man,
Through its kindling pulses ran;

Eagerly these eyes looked forth,
Questioning the teeming earth
For its stores of truth and worth;

Head and heart with schemes were rife,
Longing for some noble strife,
Planning for some perfect life.

But the Father's love decreed
Other work and other meed,
And by ways unsought did lead;

Turned aside the out-stretched hand,
Bade the feet inactive stand,
Checked the task that thought had planned;

And on eyes that loved to gaze
Upon light's intensest rays,
Dropped a veil of gentlest haze.

How the musing spirit burned!
How the wilful nature yearned,
And its sacred limits spurned!

Known, O Father, unto thee
All the long captivity
Of the soul at last set free;

And how hard it was to see
Thy great harvests silently
Whitening upon land and lea;

And to watch the reapers' throng,
Filling all the vales with song,
As they bore their sheaves along.

And to thee, O pitying God,
Known thy grace that overflowed
All that still and sacred road,

Where thy patience brought relief,
Following in thy path of grief,
Thou of suffering souls the chief!

Yet since thou hast stooped to say,
" Cast thy out-worn robe away,
Come and rest with me to-day, —

"Come to larger life and power,
Come to truth's unfailing dower,
Come to strength renewed each hour ; " —

To the dear ones gathered here
Make thy loving purpose clear,
And thy light shine round this bier.
Eliza Scudder.

Pass Over to Thy Rest.

From this bleak hill of storms,
To yon warm, sunny heights,
Where love forever shines,
    Pass over to thy rest,
    The rest of God!

From hunger and from thirst,
From toil and weariness,
From shadows and from dreams,
    Pass over to thy rest,
    The rest of God!

From weakness and from pain,
From trembling and from strife,
From watching and from fears,
    Pass over to thy rest,
    The rest of God!

From vanity and lies,
From mockery and snares,
From disappointed hopes,
    Pass over to thy rest,
    The rest of God!

From unrealities,
From hollow scenes of change,
From ache and emptiness,
    Pass over to thy rest,
    The rest of God!

From this unanchored world,
Whose morrow none can tell,
From all things restless here,
    Pass over to thy rest,
    The rest of God!

H. Bonar.

A Prisoner.

If one had watched a prisoner many a year,
Standing beside a barrèd window-pane,
Fettered with heavy hand-cuffs and with chain,
And gazing on the blue sky far and clear;
And suddenly some morning we should hear
The man had in the night contrived to gain
His freedom and was safe, would that bring pain?
Ah! would it not to dullest heart appear
Good tidings? Yesterday I looked on one
Who lay as if asleep in perfect peace.
His long imprisonment for life was done;
Eternity's great freedom his release
Had brought, yet they who loved him called him dead,
And wept, refusing to be comforted.

H. H.

The Border-Lands.

Father, into thy loving hands
  My feeble spirit I commit,
While wandering in these Border-Lands,
  Until thy voice shall summon it.

Father, I would not dare to choose
  A longer life, an earlier death;
I know not what my soul might lose
  By shortened or protracted breath.

These Border-Lands are calm and still,
    And solemn are their silent shades;
And my heart welcomes them, until
    The light of life's long evening fades.

I hear them spoken of with dread,
    As fearful and unquiet places;
Shades, where the living and the dead
    Look sadly in each other's faces.

But since thy hand hath led me here,
    And I have seen the Border-Land;
Seen the dark river flowing near,
    Stood on its brink, as now I stand;

There has been nothing to alarm
    My trembling soul; how could I fear
While thus encircled with thine arm?
    I never felt thee half so near.

What should appal me in a place
    That brings me hourly nearer thee?
When I may almost see thy face —
    Surely 'tis here my soul would be.
                  Euphemia Saxby.

Rest.

I lay me down to sleep,
    With little thought or care
Whether my waking find
    Me here, or there.

A bowing, burdened head,
    That only asks to rest,
Unquestioning, upon
    A loving breast.

My good right hand forgets
    Its cunning now;
To march the weary march
    I know not how.

I am not eager, bold,
 Nor strong — all that is past;
I am ready not to do
 At last, at last.

My half day's work is done,
 And this is all my part;
I give a patient God
 My patient heart,

And grasp his banner still,
 Though all its blue be dim;
These stripes, no less than stars,
 Lead after him.
Anonymous.

Free.

What did we ask with all our love for him,
But just a breath of fuller life
To ease the laboring lungs? And God hath given him
The gift of life itself, — full, everlasting life!
What did we pray for? Rest even for one night,
That he might rise with sleep's most golden dews,
Refreshed to feel the morning in his soul;
And God hath given him his eternal rest!
We could not proffer freedom for one hour
From that dread weight of weariness he bore,
Struggling for years to shake death's shadow off;
And God hath made him free forevermore!
Gerald Massey.

Sleeping and Waking

Sleep, tired one, sleep!
Earth's wakefulness hath pain and sore unrest,
And joys and sorrows battling in the breast,
 nd good that is but longing for the best.
 Sleep, tired one, sleep!

   Sleep, lovely one, sleep!
Earth's beauty is a summer sunset's glow,
Fading to darkness as the night shades grow;
Thy beauty was of climes we do not know.
   Sleep, lovely one, sleep!

   Sleep, loving one, sleep!
  Warm hearts and tender cluster, true and kind;
Thy sorrowing ones they shall not fail to find;
Love well shall guard the love thou leav'st behind.
   Sleep, loving one, sleep!

   Sleep, beloved one, sleep!
Thy dear sweet memory in our hearts abides;
More dear and sweet as time more swiftly glides,
Most dear, most sweet, for that to which it guides.
   Sleep, beloved one, sleep!

   Wake, deathless one, wake!
The Life thou lovedst loves thee still for aye;
It had no kinship with thy perishing clay,
But crowns thy forehead with eternal Day:
Thou waitest for thine own — lighting the way.
   Wake, deathless one, wake.
      F. E. Abbot (to E. C. Potter.)

Sleep.

He sees when their footsteps falter, when their hearts grow weak and faint;
He marks when their strength is failing, and listens to each complaint;
He bids them rest for a season, for the path-way has grown too steep;
And folded in fair green pastures, he giveth his loved ones sleep.

Like weary and worn-out children, that sigh for the daylight's close,
He knows that they oft are longing for home and its sweet repose;
So he calls them in from their labors ere the shadows around them creep,
And silently watching o'er them, he giveth his loved ones sleep.

He giveth it, oh! so gently, as a mother will hush to rest
The babe that she softly pillows so tenderly on her breast;
Forgotten are now the trials and sorrows that made them weep,
For with many a soothing promise, he giveth his loved ones sleep.

He giveth it! Friends the dearest can never this boon bestow;
But he touches the drooping eyelids, and placid the features grow;
Their foes may gather about them, and storms may round them sweep,
But, guarding them safe from danger, he giveth his loved ones sleep.

All dread of the distant future, all fears that oppressed to-day,
Like mists that clear in the sunlight, have noiselessly passed away;
Nor call, nor clamor can rouse them from slumbers so pure and deep,
For only his voice can reach them, who giveth his loved ones sleep.

Weep not that their toils are over, weep not that their race is run;
God grant we may rest as calmly when our work, like theirs, is done!
Till then we would yield with gladness our treasures to him to keep,
And rejoice in the sweet assurance, he giveth his loved ones sleep.

Anonymous.

Our Home Maker.

Where the mountains slope to the westward,
    And their purple chalices hold
The new made wine of the sunset —
    Crimson and amber and gold —

In this old, wide-opened doorway,
    With the elm-boughs over head —
The house all garnished behind her,
    And the plentiful table spread —

She has stood to welcome our coming,
    Watching our upward climb,
In the sweet June weather that brought us,
    Oh, many and many a time!

To-day, in the gentle splendor
    Of the early summer noon —
Perfect in sunshine and fragrance
    Although it is hardly June —

SUFFERING AND REST.

Again is the doorway opened,
    And the house is garnished and sweet;
But she silently waits for our coming,
    And we enter with silent feet.

A little within she is waiting,
    Not where she has met us before;
For over the pleasant threshold
    She is only to cross once more.

The smile on her face is quiet,
    And a lily is on her breast;
Her hands are folded together
    And the word on her lips is "rest."

And yet it looks like a welcome,
    For her work is compassed and done;
All things are seemly and ready,
    And her summer is just begun.

It is we who may not cross over:
    Only with song and prayer,
A little way into the glory,
    We may reach as we leave her there.

But we cannot think of her idle;
    She must be a home-maker still;
God giveth that work to the angels
    Who fittest the task fulfil;

And somewhere, yet, in the hilltops
    Of the country that hath no pain,
She will watch in her beautiful doorway,
    To bid us a welcome again.

                  A. D. T. Whitney.

Tired Out.

He does well who does his best;
Is he weary? let him rest.
Brothers! I have done my best,
I am weary — let me rest.

After toiling oft in vain,
Baffled, yet to struggle fain,
After toiling long to gain
Little good with weary pain,
Let me rest. But lay me low
Where the hedge-side roses blow,
Where the little daisies grow,
Where the winds a-maying go,
Where the foot-path rustics plod,
Where the breeze-bowed poplars nod,
Where the old woods worship God,
Where his pencil paints the sod,
Where the wedded throstle sings,
Where the young bird tries his wings,
Where at times the tempests roar,
Shaking distant sea and shore,
To be heard by me no more!
There beneath the breezy west,
Tired and thankful, let me rest
Like a child that sleepeth best
On its mother's gentle breast.

Anonymous.

Disenthralled.

Dead! Do you say that he is dead?
  Take back the word, it is not true!
An empty cage, you might have said,
  Has lost the singer that we knew —
The song rose level with the stars,
That charmed us even in prison bars.

But dead? There can be no such word
  For that which was serenely bright,
Made in the image of the Lord,
  An effluence from the central light,
An inbreathed essence from on high,
A heaven-lit spark! that could not die.

Not dead — but free — he soars above
  The limit of our lesser scope,

And we, because we shared his love,
　May cherish the uplifting hope
That life to us is more, by just
　His altitude above our dust.

More by the power he has attained
　To minister as angels may;
More by the knowledge he has gained
　Of love's supremest, patient way;
Of blessing through the cloud or sun,
So one all-perfect Will be done.

And he (the thought is radiant) he
　This very moment may be near,
With solace meted soothingly
　To feed a hope or hush a fear:
So true it is, divinest things
Come borne to us on hidden wings.

So well we knew our Father's care
　Hovers about us, night and day,
So sweet it is to think the air
　Is moved in a mysterious way
By breath of one beloved on earth
Grown lovelier by celestial birth.

Then say not he is of the dead,
　'Tis only we in cerements dim,
Who fail of life around, o'erhead;
　But say it nevermore of him
Whom death to livelier joys has called,
Who lives among us disenthralled.

Mary B. Dodge.

The Conqueror's Grave.

Within this lowly grave a conqueror lies,
And yet the monument proclaims it not.
　A simple name alone,
　To the great world unknown,
Is graven here, and wild-flowers rising round,
Meek meadow-sweet, and violets of the ground,
　Lean lovingly against the humble stone.

SUFFERING AND REST.

Here in the quiet earth, they laid apart
No man of iron mould and bloody hands,
But one of tender spirit and delicate frame;
    Gentlest in mien and mind
    Of gentle womankind,
Timidly shrinking from the breath of blame:
One in whose eyes the smile of kindness made
Its haunt, like flowers by sunny brooks in May;
Yet at the thought of others' pain a shade
Of sweeter sadness chased the smile away.

Nor deem that when the hand that moulders here
Was raised in menace, realms were chilled with fear.
Not thus were waged the mighty wars that gave
The victory to her who fills this grave:
    Alone her task was wrought,
    Alone the battle fought;
Through that long strife her constant hope was staid
On God alone, nor looked for other aid.

She met the hosts of Sorrow with a look
   That altered not beneath the frown they wore,
And soon the lowering brood were tamed, and took,
   Meekly, her gentle rule and frowned no more.
Her soft hand put aside the assaults of wrath,
    And calmly broke in twain
    The fiery shafts of pain,
And rent the nets of passion from her path.
  By that victorious hand dispair was slain;
With love she vanquished hate and overcame
   Evil with good in her great Master's name.

O gentle sleeper, from thy grave I go
   Consoled, though sad, in hope and yet in fear.
    Brief is the time, I know,
    The warfare scarce begun;
Yet all may win the triumphs thou hast won.
  Still flows the fount whose waters strengthened thee;
The victors' names are yet too few to fill
   Heaven's mighty roll; the glorious armory,
That ministered to thee, is open still.
William C. Bryant.

PART V.

CHILDHOOD — YOUTH.

Sowing in Tears.

Straight and still the baby lies,
No more smiling in his eyes,
Neither tears nor wailing cries.

Smiles and tears alike are done;
He has need of neither one —
Only, I must weep alone.

Tiny fingers, all too slight,
Hold within their grasping tight,
Waxen berries scarce more white.

Nights and days of weary pain
I have held them close — in vain;
Now I never shall again.

Crossed upon a silent breast,
By no suffering distressed,
Here they lie in marble rest.

They shall ne'er unfolded be,
Never more in agony
Cling so pleadingly to me.

Yearning sore, I only know
I am very full of woe —
And I want my baby so!

Weary heart, that thou should'st prove
So unworthy of the love
Which thy darling doth remove!

Blinded eyes, that cannot see
Past the present misery,
Joy and comfort full and free!

O my Father! loving Lord!
Give me shame at my own word,
Strength and patience me afford.

I will yield me to thy will;
Now thy purposes fulfil;
Only help me to be still.

Though the mother-heart shall ache,
I believe that, for his sake,
It shall not entirely break.

And I know I yet shall own,
For my seeds of sorrow sown,
Sheaves of joy around thy throne!

Anonymous.

Our White Dove.

A white dove out of heaven flew,
   White as the whitest shape of grace
   That nestles in the soft embrace
Of heaven when skies are summer blue;

It came with dew-drop purity,
   On glad wings of the morning light,
   And sank into our life, so white
A vision! sweetly, secretly!

Our dove had eyes of Baby blue,
   Soft as the speedwell's by the way,
   That looketh up as it would say,
"Who kissed me while I slept, did you?"

It seemed to come from far green fields
   To meet us over life's rough sea,
   With leaf of promise from the tree
In which a dearer nest it builds.

We held it as the leaves of life
   In hidden silent service fold
   About a Rose's heart of gold,
So jealous of all outer strife!

One day she pined up in our face
   With a low cry we could not still,
   A moaning we could never heal,
For sleep in some more quiet place.

The look grew pleading in her eyes,
   And mournful as the lonesome light
   That in a window burns all night,
Asking for stillness, when one dies.

The hand of Death so coldly clings,
   So strongly draws the weak life-wave
   Into his dark, vast, silent cave;
Our little Dove must use its wings!

And so it sought the dearer nest;
   A little way across the sea
   It kept us wingèd company,
Then sank into its leafier rest.

And left us day by day to feel
   A sadness in the sweetest words,
   A broken heartstring mid the chords,
A tone more tremulous when we kneel.

The stars that shone in her dear eyes
   May be a little while withdrawn
   To rise and lead the eternal dawn
For us, up heaven in other skies.

Our bird of God but soars and sings:
   Oft when life's heaving wave's at rest,
   She makes her mirror in my breast,
I feel a winnowing of wings.

Be good! and you shall find her where
  No wind can shake the wee bird's nest;
  No dreams can break the wee bird's rest
No night, no pain, no parting there!

No echoes of old storms gone by!
  Earth's sorrows slumber peacefully;
  The weary are at rest, and He
Shall wipe the tears from every eye.
Gerald Massey.

An Infant's Death.

A snow-flake falls, from out the air above,
Upon some spot of ground where lingers yet
The warmth of Summer's and of Autumn's sun;
And in a moment it has passed from sight.
Most beautiful its crystal shape, a six-
Rayed star, well fitted, if it could have stayed
Until the sunlight fell thereon, to give
A wealth of rainbow-hues, to gladden all
Who saw its loveliness. Why came the flake
Of snow, to go so soon, and leave no trace?
A useless birth, a useless death, it seems.

So seems — but when we trace the snow-flake back,
And try to image all the wondrous store
Of nature's skill in that one bit displayed,
And know how all things joined together are,
And work in harmony in this great world,
So that from furthest parts the forces come,
Which meet an instant, give the snow-flake birth,
Then pass to other work — we know what seems
A trifling thing, is far from being so;
In one grand thought the truth comes home to us,
That, were it not the snow-flake came to earth,
The world could not have been the same to-day.

So, when from out the unknown space, there comes
A little child to earth, which melts too soon
From out the lap which gave it birth away,
Before the sunlight love of home could give
It consciousness of life — at once we ask,
Why came the babe at all, so soon to go?
A useless birth, a useless death, it seems.

So seems — but when we gather up the threads,
The myriad threads, which bind its little life
To lives of countless thousands gone before,
To lives of countless thousands yet to come, —
E'en as the rippling wave will reach at last
From hither unto farther shore, and move,
With felt or unfelt touch, all things that float
Upon the surface of the watery deep, —
We know, with faith beyond the power of sight,
That not in vain the little one did come,
Did stay awhile, then pass from sight away;
The world — our world at least — is not the same
As though the babe had never come to us.
Rowland Connor.

A Baby's Death.

The little feet that never trod
   Earth, never strayed in field or street,
What hand leads upward back to God
      The little feet?

Their pilgrimage's period
   A few swift moons have seen complete
Since mother's hands first clasped and shod
      The little feet.

The little hands that never sought
   Earth's prizes, worthless all as sands,
What gift has death, God's servant, brought
      The little hands?

Ere this, perchance, though love knows naught,
  Flowers fill them, grown in lovelier lands,
Where hands of guiding angels caught
  The little hands.

The little eyes that never knew
  Light other than of dawning skies,
What new life now lights up anew
  The little eyes?

No storm, we know, may change the blue,
  Soft heaven that haply death descries;
No tears like these in ours, bedew
  The little eyes.
                                A. C. Swinburne.

The Two Mysteries.

[In the middle of the room, in its white coffin, lay the dead child, nephew of the poet. Near it, in a great chair, sat Walt Whitman, surrounded by little ones, and holding a beautiful little girl in his lap. The child looked curiously at the spectacle of death, and then inquiringly into the old man's face. "You don't know what it is, do you, my dear?" said he. "We don't either."

We know not what it is, dear, this sleep so deep and still;
The folded hands, the awful calm, the cheek so pale and chill;
The lids that will not lift again, though we may call and call;
The strange, white solitude of peace that settles over all.

We know not what it means, dear, this desolate heart-pain, —
This dread to take our daily way, and walk in it again.
We know not to what other sphere the loved who leave us go;
Nor why we're left to wonder still; nor why we do not know.

But this we know: our loved and dead, if they should come this
    day, —
Should come and ask us, "What is life?" not one of us could say.
Life is a mystery as deep as ever death can be;
Yet, oh, how sweet it is to us, this life we live and see!

Then might they say, — these vanished ones, — and blessed is the
   thought! —
" So death is sweet to us, beloved, though we may tell you naught:
We may not tell it to the quick, — this mystery of death, —
Ye may not tell us, if ye would, the mystery of breath."

The child who enters life comes not with knowledge or intent,
So those who enter death must go as little children sent.
Nothing is known. But I believe that God is overhead;
And as life is to the living, so death is to the dead.
Mary Mapes Dodge.

God's Messengers.

Children are God's apostles, day by day
Sent forth to preach of love, and hope, and peace;
Nor hath thy babe his mission left undone.
To me, at least, his going hence hath given
Serener thoughts and nearer to the skies,
And opened a new fountain in my heart
For thee, my friend, and all: and oh, if Death
More near approaches, meditates, and clasps,
Even now some dearer, more reluctant hand,
God, strengthen thou my faith, that I may see
That 't is thine angel who, with loving haste,
Unto the service of the inner shrine,
Doth waken thy belovèd with a kiss.
J. R. Lowell. On the Death of a Friend's Child.

She Is Not Dead, But Sleepeth.

The baby wept;
The mother took it from the nurse's arms,
And soothed its griefs, and stilled its vain alarms,
   And baby slept.

Again it weeps,
And God doth take it from the mother's arms,
From present pain, and future unknown harms,
   And baby sleeps.
Dr. Hinds.

For a Friend in Sorrow.

It was a tender hand that drew my boy away,
Out of earth's shadow into heaven's day;
It was a loving voice that called him home,
I catch its distant music, — "Darling — come!"

I know he lives with angels now, my boy,
He sees their radiant faces, feels their joy;
And heaven is dearer, nearer and so fair,
Since this dear treasure of my heart is there.

And yet my arms are empty — oh! to hold
His face against my bosom as of old,
To clasp him close and feel the tender bliss
Of his warm nestling touch, and baby kiss.

Lord, help me if I sometimes wonder why
The message came for him and passed me by,
And marvel in my sad perplexity
How he can be content away from me!

His little life was woven close with mine
As vines in summer meet and intertwine,
So when the summons came for us to part,
The severing touch, though tender, broke my heart.

Yet dearest Lord, I will not long repine,
My bleeding heart shall find its balm in thine,
In the dark shadows I will feel for thee
And trust thee — as my baby trusted me.
Anonymous.

The Reaper and the Flowers.

There is a Reaper whose name is Death,
   And, with his sickle keen,
He reaps the bearded grain at a breath,
   And the flowers that grow between.

"Shall I have naught that is fair?" saith he;
  "Have naught but the bearded grain?
Though the breath of these flowers is sweet to me,
  I will give them all back again."

He gazed at the flowers with tearful eyes,
  He kissed their drooping leaves;
It was for the Lord of Paradise
  He bound them in his sheaves.

"My Lord has need of these flowerets gay,"
  The Reaper said, and smiled;
"Dear tokens of the earth are they,
  Where he was once a child."

"They shall all bloom in fields of light,
  Transplanted by my care,
And saints upon their garments white,
  These sacred blossoms wear."

And the mother gave, in tears and pain,
  The flowers she most did love;
She knew she should find them all again
  In the fields of light above.

Oh, not in cruelty, not in wrath,
  The Reaper came that day;
'Twas an angel visited the green earth,
  And took the flowers away.

H. W. Longfellow.

The Alpine Sheep.

After our child's untroubled breath
  Up to the Father took its way,
And on our home the shade of death
  Like a long twilight haunting lay;

And friends came round, with us to weep
  Her little spirit's swift remove,—
The story of the Alpine sheep
  Was told to us by one we love.

They, in the valley's sheltering care,
   Soon crop the meadow's tender prime,
And when the sod grows brown and bare
   The shepherd strives to make them climb

To airy shelves of pastures green,
   That hang along the mountain's side,
Where grass and flowers together lean,
   And down through mists the sunbeams slide.

But nought can tempt the timid things
   The steep and rugged path to try,
Though sweet the shepherd calls and sings,
   And seared below the pastures lie, —

Till in his arms their lambs he takes,
   Along the dizzy verge to go,
Then, heedless of the rifts and breaks,
   They follow on, o'er rock and snow.

And in those pastures, lifted fair,
   More dewy soft than lowland mead,
The shepherd drops his tender care,
   And sheep and lambs together feed.

This parable, by nature breathed,
   Blew on me as the south wind free
O'er frozen brooks, that flow unsheathed
   From icy thraldom to the sea.

A blissful vision, through the night,
   Would all my happy senses sway,
Of the good shepherd on the height,
   Or climbing up the stony way,

Holding *our* little lamb asleep,
   While, like the murmur of the sea,
Sounded that voice along the deep,
   Saying " Arise, and follow me ! "

                                Maria Lowell.

Little Children

In the baron's hall of pride,
By the poor man's dull fireside,
'Mid the mighty, 'mid the mean,
Little children may be seen,
Like the flowers that spring up fair,
Bright and countless everywhere!

Blessings on them! they in me
Move a kindly sympathy,
With their wishes, hopes and fears;
With their laughter and their tears;
With their wonder so intense,
And their small experience!

Little children, not alone
On this wide earth are ye known;
'Mid its labors and its cares,
'Mid its sufferings and its snares;
Free from sorrow, free from strife,
In the world of love and life,
Where no sinful thing hath trod —
In the presence of your God,
Spotless, blameless, glorified —
Little children, ye abide.

Mary Howitt.

Buried To-Day.

Buried to-day;
  When the soft green buds are bursting out,
  And up on the south-wind comes a shout
Of village boys and girls at play
In the mild spring evening gray.

Taken away;
  Sturdy of heart and stout of limb,
  From eyes that drew half their light from him,
And put low, low underneath the clay,
In his spring, — on this spring day.

Passes away,
　All the pride of boy-life begun,
　All the hope of life yet to run;
Who dares to question when One saith "Nay."
Murmur not, — only pray

Enters to-day,
　Another body in church-yard sod,
　Another soul on the life in God.
His Christ was buried — and lives alway;
Trust him and go your way.

　　　　　　　　　D. M. Mulock-Craik.

The Changeling.

I had a little daughter,
　And she was given to me
To lead me gently backward
　To the heavenly Father's knee,
That I by the force of nature,
　Might, in some dim wise, divine
The depth of his infinite patience
　To this wayward soul of mine.

I know not how others saw her,
　But to me she was wholly fair,
And the light of the heaven she came from
　Still lingered and gleamed in her hair;
For it was as wavy and golden,
　And as many changes took,
As the shadows of sun-gilt ripples
　On the yellow bed of a brook.

She had been with us scarce a twelvemonth,
　And it hardly seemed a day,
When a troop of wandering angels
　Stole my little daughter away;
Or perhaps those heavenly guardians
　But loosed the hampering strings,
And when they had opened her cage door
　My little bird used her wings.

But they left in her stead a changeling,
  A little angel child,
That seems like a bud in full blossom,
  And smiles as she never smiled.
This child is not mine as the first was,
  I cannot sing it to rest,
I cannot lift it up fatherly
  And bliss it upon my breast;
Yet it lies in my little one's cradle,
  And sits in my little one's chair,
And the light of the heaven she's gone to
  Transfigures its golden hair.
J. R. Lowell.

The Chamber Over the Gate.

Is it so far from thee
Thou canst no longer see,
In the Chamber over the Gate,
That old man desolate,
Weeping and wailing sore
For his son, who is no more?
  O Absalom, my son!

Is it so long ago
That cry of human woe
From the walled city came,
Calling on his dear name,
That it has died away
In the distance of to-day?
  O Absalom, my son!

There is no far or near,
There is neither there nor here,
There is neither soon nor late,
In that Chamber over the Gate,
Nor any long ago
To that cry of human woe,
  O Absalom, my son!

Somewhere at every hour
The watchman on the tower
Looks forth, and sees the fleet
Approach of the hurrying feet
Of messengers, that bear
The tidings of despair.
  O Absalom, my son!

He goes forth from the door,
Who shall return no more.
With him our joy departs;
The light goes out in our hearts;
In the Chamber over the Gate
We sit disconsolate.
  O Absalom, my son!

That 't is a common grief
Bringeth but slight relief;
Ours is the bitterest loss,
Ours is the heaviest cross;
And forever the cry will be
" Would God I had died for thee,
  O Absalom, my son!"

H. W. Longfellow.

My Child.

I cannot make him dead!
His fair sunshiny head
Is ever bounding round my study chair;
  Yet when my eyes, now dim
  With tears, I turn to him,
The vision vanishes, — he is not there!

  I walk my parlor floor,
  And, through the open door,
I hear a footfall on the chamber stair;
  I 'm stepping toward the hall
  To give the boy a call;
And then bethink me that — he is not there!

> I know his face is hid
> Under the coffin lid,
> Closed are his eyes; cold is his forehead fair;
> My hand that marble felt;
> O'er it in prayer I knelt;
> Yet my heart whispers that — he is not there!
>
> Not there! Where, then, is he?
> The form I used to see
> Was but the raiment that he used to wear.
> The grave, that now doth press
> Upon that cast-off dress,
> Is but his wardrobe locked; he is not there!
>
> He lives! — in all the past
> He lives; nor to the last,
> Of seeing him again will I despair;
> In dreams I see him now;
> And, on his angel brow,
> I see it written, "Thou shalt see me *there!*"
>
> Yes, we all live to God!
> Father, thy chastening rod
> So help us, thine afflicted ones, to bear,
> That, in the spirit land,
> Meeting at thy right hand,
> 'Twill be our heaven to find that — he is there.
>
> *John Pierpont.*

The Morning-Glory.

> We wreathed about our darling's head
>   The morning-glory bright;
> Her little face looked out beneath
>   So full of life and light,
> So lit, as with a sunrise,
>   That we could only say,
> "She is the morning-glory true,
>   And her poor types are they."

So always from that happy time
  We called her by their name,
And very fitting did it seem, —
  For, sure as morning came,
Behind her cradle bars she smiled
  To catch the first faint ray,
As from the trellis smiles the flower,
  And opens to the day.

We used to think how she had come,
  Even as comes the flower,
The last and perfect added gift
  To crown Love's morning hour;
And how in her was imaged forth
  The love we could not say,
As on the little dewdrops round
  Shines back the heart of day.

The morning-glory's blossoming
  Will soon be coming round, —
We see their rows of heart-shaped leaves
  Upspringing from the ground;
The tender things the winter killed
  Renew again their birth,
But the glory of our morning
  Has passed away from earth.

Earth! in vain our aching eyes
  Stretch over thy green plain!
Too harsh thy dews, too gross thine air,
  Her spirit to sustain;
But up in groves of Paradise
  Full surely we shall see
Our morning-glory beautiful
  Twine round our dear Lord's knee.

Maria Lowell.

Gone.

Another hand is beckoning us,
  Another call is given;
And glows once more with angel-steps
  The path which reaches heaven.

Our young and gentle friend, whose smile
  Made brighter summer hours,
Amid the frosts of autumn time,
  Has left us with the flowers.

The light of her young life went down,
  As sinks behind the hill
The glory of a setting star, —
  Clear, suddenly, and still.

As pure and sweet, her fair brow seemed
  Eternal as the sky;
And, like the brook's low song, her voice, —
  A sound which could not die.

And half we deemed she needed not
  The changing of her sphere,
To give to heaven a shining one,
  Who walked an angel here.

The blessing of her quiet life
  Fell on us like the dew;
And good thoughts where her footsteps pressed,
  Like fairy blossoms grew.

Sweet promptings unto kindest deeds
  Were in her very look;
We read her face as one who reads
  A true and holy book.

We miss her in her place of prayer,
  And by the hearth-fire's light;
We pause beside her door to hear
  Once more her sweet " Good-Night ! "

There seems a shadow on the day,
  Her smile no longer cheers ;
A dimness on the stars of night,
  Like eyes that look through tears.

Alone unto our Father's will
  One thought hath reconciled;
That he whose love exceedeth ours
  Hath taken home his child.

Fold her, O Father! in thine arms,
  And let her henceforth be
A messenger of love between
  Our human hearts and thee.

Still let her mild rebuking stand
  Between us and the wrong,
And her dear memory serve to make
  Our faith in goodness strong.

And grant that she, who, trembling here,
  Distrusted all her powers,
May welcome to her holier home
  The well-beloved of ours.

J. G. Whittier.

We Watched Her Breathing.

We watched her breathing through the night,
  Her breathing soft and low,
As in her breast the wave of life
  Kept heaving to and fro.

So silently we seemed to speak,
  So slowly moved about,
As we had lent her half our powers
  To eke her living out.

Our very hopes belied our fears,
  Our fears our hopes belied, —
We thought her dying when she slept,
  And sleeping when she died.

For when the morn came dim and sad,
   And chill with early showers,
Her quiet eyelids closed, — she had
   Another morn than ours.
Thomas Hood.

The Lent Jewels.

In schools of wisdom all the day was spent;
His steps at eve the Rabbi homeward bent,
With homeward thoughts which dwelt upon the wife
And two fair children who consoled his life:
She, meeting at the threshold, led him in,
And with the words preventing did begin, —
" Ever rejoicing at your wished return,
Yet do I most so now; for since this morn
I have been much perplexed and sorely tried
Upon one point which you shall now decide.

" Some years ago a friend into my care
Some jewels gave; rich precious gems they were;
But having given them in my charge, this friend
Did afterward nor come for them nor send,
But left them in my keeping for so long
That now it almost seems to me a wrong
That he should suddenly arrive to-day
To take those jewels which he left, away.
What think you? Shall I freely yield them back,
And with no murmuring — so henceforth to lack
Those gems myself, which I had learned to see
Almost as mine forever, mine in fee?"
" What question can be here? Your own true heart
Must needs advise you of the only part;
That may be claimed again which was but lent,
And should be yielded without discontent;
Nor surely can we find herein a wrong,
That it was left us to enjoy it long."

"Good is the word," she answered. " May we now
And evermore that it is good allow ! "
And rising, to an inner chamber led,
And there she showed him, stretched upon one bed,
Two children pale ; and he the jewels knew
Which God had lent him and resumed anew.

R. C. Trench.

Resignation.

There is no flock, however watched and tended,
    But one dead lamb is there !
There is no fireside, howsoe'er defended,
    But has one vacant chair !

The air is full of farewells to the dying,
    And mournings for the dead ;
The heart of Rachel, for her children crying,
    Will not be comforted !

Let us be patient ! These severe afflictions
    Not from the ground arise,
But oftentimes celestial benedictions
    Assume this dark disguise.

We see but dimly through the mists and vapors ;
    Amid these earthly damps,
What seem to us but sad, funereal tapers
    May be heaven's distant lamps.

There is no Death ! What seems so is transition ;
    This life of mortal breath
Is but a suburb of the life elysian,
    Whose portal we call Death.

She is not dead, — the child of our affection, —
    But gone unto that school
Where she no longer needs our poor protection,
    And Christ himself doth rule.

In that great cloister's stillness and seclusion,
    By guardian angels led,
Safe from temptation, safe from sin's pollution,
    She lives, whom we call dead.

Day after day, we think what she is doing
  In those bright realms of air;
Year after year, her tender steps pursuing,
  Behold her grown more fair.

Thus do we walk with her, and keep unbroken
  The bond which nature gives,
Thinking that our remembrance, though unspoken,
  May reach her where she lives.

Not as a child shall we again behold her;
  For, when with raptures wild
In our embraces we again enfold her,
  She will not be a child,

But a fair maiden, in her Father's mansion,
  Clothed with celestial grace;
And beautiful with all the soul's expansion
  Shall we behold her face.

And though, at times, impetuous with emotion
  And anguish long suppressed,
The swelling heart heaves, moaning like the ocean
  That cannot be at rest, —

We will be patient, and assuage the feeling
  We may not wholly stay;
By silence sanctifying, not concealing,
  The grief that must have way.

H. W. Longfellow.

Vesta.

O Christ of God! whose life and death
  Our own have reconciled,
Most quietly, most tenderly,
  Take home this little child!

Thy grace is in her patient eyes,
  Thy words are on her tongue;
The very silence round her seems
  As if the angels sung.

Her smile is as a listening child's
  Who hears its mother call;
The lilies of thy perfect peace
  About her pillow fall.

She leans from out our clinging arms
  To rest herself in thine;
Alone to thee, dear Lord, can we
  Our well-beloved resign!

Oh, less for her than for ourselves
  We bow our heads and pray;
Her setting star, like Bethlehem's
  To thee shall point the way.

J. G. Whittier.

Lifted Over.

As tender mothers guiding baby steps,
Where places come at which the tiny feet
Would trip, lift up the little ones in arms
Of love, and set them down beyond the harm,
So did our Father watch the precious boy,
Led o'er the stones by me, who stumbled oft
Myself, but strove to help my darling on :
He saw the sweet limbs faltering, and saw
Rough ways before us, where my arms would fail;
So reached from heaven, and lifting the dear child,
Who smiled in leaving me, he put him down,
Beyond all hurt, beyond my sight, and bade
Him wait for me! Shall I not then be glad,
And, thanking God, press on to overtake?

H. H.

PART VI.

THE AGED.

The Good Grandmother.

Fold reverently the weary hands
   That toiled so long and well;
And while your tears of sorrow fall
   Let sweet thanksgivings swell.

That life-work stretching o'er long years
   A varied web has been;
With silver strands by sorrow wrought,
   And sunny gleams between.

How bright she always made the home!
   It seemed as if the floor
Was always flecked with spots of sun,
   And barred with brightness o'er.

The very falling of her step
   Made music as she went;
A loving song was on her lip,
   The song of full content.

O gently fold the weary hands
   That toiled so long and well!
The spirit rose to angel bands,
   When off earth's mantle fell.

She's safe within her Father's house
   Where many mansions be;
O pray that thus such rest may come
   Dear hearts, to thee and me!

Anonymous.

Beautiful Hands.

Such beautiful, beautiful hands!
    They're neither white nor small,
And you, I know, would scarcely think
    That they were fair at all.
I've looked on hands whose form and hue
    A sculptor's dream might be,
Yet are those aged wrinkled hands
    Most beautiful to me.

Such beautiful, beautiful hands!
    Though the heart was weary and sad,
These patient hands kept toiling on,
    That the children might be glad.
I almost weep, as looking back
    To childhood's distant day,
I think how these hands rested not
    When mine were at their play.

Such beautiful, beautiful hands!
    They're growing feeble now;
For time and pain have left their mark
    On hand and heart and brow.
Alas! Alas! the nearing time,
    And the sad, sad day to me,
When 'neath the daisies, out of sight,
    These hands will folded be.

But oh, beyond this shadow-lamp,
    Where all is bright and fair,
I know full well these dear old hands
    Will palms of victory bear.
Where crystal streams, through endless years,
    Flow over golden sands,
And where the old grow young again,
    I'll clasp my mother's hands.

Ellen H. M. Gates.

Homeward.

They sat in peace in the sunshine,
   Till the day was almost done,
And then, at its close, an angel
   Stole over the threshold-stone.

He folded their hands together;
   He touched their eyelids with balm,
And their last breath floated outward,
   Like the close of a solemn psalm.

Perhaps in that miracle-country
   They will give her lost youth back,
And the flowers of the vanished springtime
   Will bloom in the spirit's track.

One draught from the living waters
   Shall call back his manhood's prime,
And eternal years shall measure
   The love that outlasted time.

But the shapes that they left behind them
   The wrinkles and silver hair —
Made holy to us by the kisses
   The angels hold printed there —

We will hide away 'neath the willows,
   When the day is low in the West,
Where the sunbeams cannot find them,
   Nor the winds disturb their rest.

And we'll suffer no telltale tombstone,
   With its age and date, to rise
O'er the two who are old no longer,
   In the Father's house in the skies.

          Louise Chandler Moulton.

Waiting.

She waited for the summons; lengthening days
Had ripened the rich harvest of her years;
The sun hung low; — across the level plain,
In the slant rays, ripe bent the bearded grain.
Her feet were weary, and, with faltering hands,
She bound the golden tribute of the lands.
We watched the coming night with tender fear;
She murmured to herself good words of cheer;
We followed, gleaning; toil, and heat, and dust
Forgotten, in her perfect faith and trust.
We followed, gleaning: all the night
We heard her voice thank God, in cheerful praise,
For this dear life, and all its happy days;
Then there was silence, and we found at dawn
Only the faded garments she had worn.

The Old Man's Funeral.

I saw an aged man upon his bier;
  His hair was thin and white, and on his brow
A record of the cares of many a year, —
  Cares that were ended and forgotten now.
And there was sadness round, and faces bowed,
And woman's tears fell fast, and children wailed aloud.

Then rose another hoary man, and said,
  In faltering accents to that weeping train:
" Why mourn ye that our aged friend is dead?
  Ye are not sad to see the gathered grain:
Nor when their mellow fruits the orchards cast,
Nor when the yellow woods let fall the ripened mast.

" Ye sigh not when the sun, his course fulfilled, —
  His glorious course, rejoicing earth and sky, —
In the soft evening, when the winds are stilled,
  Sinks where his islands of refreshment lie,
And leaves the smile of his departure spread
O'er the warm-colored heaven and ruddy mountain-head.

THE AGED.

"Why weep ye then for him, who, having won
  The bound of man's appointed years, at last,
Life's blessings all enjoyed, life's labors done,
  Serenely to his final rest has passed;
While the soft memory of his virtues yet
Lingers, like twilight hues when the bright sun is set.

"His youth was innocent; his riper age
  Marked with some act of goodness every day;
And watched by eyes that loved him, calm and sage,
  Faded his late declining years away:
Meekly he gave his being up and went
To share the holy rest that waits a life well spent.

"That life was happy; every day he gave
  Thanks for the fair existence that was his;
For a sick fancy made him not her slave,
  To mock him with her phantom miseries.
No chronic tortures racked his aged limbs,
For luxury and sloth had nourished none for him.

"And I am glad that he has lived thus long,
  And glad that he has gone to his reward;
Nor can I deem that Nature did him wrong,
  Softly to disengage the vital cord;
For when his hand grew palsied, and his eye
Dark with the mists of age, it was his time to die."
                                            W. C. Bryant.

The Home-Seeker.

I.

Twilight falls: a tiny maiden
  Cometh up the village street:
Vagrant locks, all dewy laden,
  Eager eyes and tired feet
Hath the shadowy little maiden.

Tired of wandering and of playing,
  Up the dim street see her come!
Hurrying now, and now delaying,
  Toward the rest and love of home,
Comes the maiden from her playing.

THE AGED.

II.

See! again! a woman hasting
   Down a shadowy, sunset way,
Loving, anxious glances casting
   Through the twilight soft and gray;
Homeward, love-ward she is hasting.

Laughing children run to meet her
   From the home-door open wide;
Loving words and kisses greet her,
   Pattering feet run by her side;
All the home comes forth to meet her.

III.

Look once more! a pilgrim weary
   Standeth in the twilight gray;
All around is strange and dreary,
   As she asks, with plaintive query,
"Can you show the homeward way?
   Lead me homeward: I am weary."

Then a Presence stood to guide her,
   Pointing where the way did lie;
Gently spoke, and walked beside her
   To a gateway dim and high.
"Home!" she breathed, with restful sigh,
To the Presence that did guide her.

IV.

Homeward still, the tiny maiden,
Motherhood, love- and care-laden,
Age, with weight of years oppressed,
Homeward turn for love and rest.
And the home, with open door,
Waits with "Welcome" evermore.

                     W. H. Savage.

INDEX OF FIRST LINES.

Poems marked thus (*) have been printed only in part.

	PAGE
After our child's untroubled breath	191
A little fold of hands	123
*All as God wills, who wisely heeds	154
All that God wounds he constantly is healing	128
*Another hand is beckoning us	199
Answer me, burning stars of night	123
A snowflake falls from out the air above	186
As tender mothers guiding baby steps	204
At eve it shall be light, the promise reads	163
*A white dove out of heaven flew	184
Beside a massive gateway built up in years gone by	110
Blindfolded and alone I wait	134
Brother, the angels say	133
Buried to-day	193
*Children are God's Apostles	189
Climbing the mountain's shaggy crest	117
Come forth, come forth with solemn song	114
Dead! do you say that he is dead?	180
Drifting away like mote on the stream	135
*Dropping down the troubled river	112
Dust to dust, the heart makes cry	136
*Farewell! since nevermore for thee	129
Father, before thy footstool kneeling	149
Father, into thy loving hands	174
*Fear death? — to feel the fog in my throat	130

INDEX.

	PAGE
*Fold reverently the weary hands	205
From this bleak hill of storms	173
Gentle friends, who gather here	171
*God gives us love; something to love	161
*God giveth quietness at last	131
God of the living, in whose eyes	126
Good-bye, till morning comes again	153
He does well who does his best	179
*He has done the work of a true man	161
He sees when their footsteps falter	177
He who died at Azan sends	119
*Her still and quiet life flowed on	160
*I cannot, cannot say	140
*I cannot make him dead	196
I cannot think of them as dead	139
*I do not come to weep above thy pall	157
If one had watched a prisoner many a year	174
*" If ye loved me," Jesus said	165
I had a little daughter	194
I hear it singing, singing sweetly	148
I lay me down to rest	175
I like that ancient Saxon phrase	118
In schools of wisdom all the day was spent	201
*In the Baron's hall of pride	193
Into the silent land	126
I saw an aged man upon his bier	208
Is it so far from thee?	195
I think if thou couldst know	148
I think it is over, over	170
It singeth low in every heart	116
It was a tender hand that drew my boy away	190
*I will not mock thee with the poor world's common	155
I will not think the last farewell we hear	152
Life and thought have gone away	113
Life! I know not what thou art	129
Life of our life, and light of all our seeing	150

INDEX.

*Nothing is our own, we hold our treasure 121

O blessed life of service and of love 164
O Christ of God! whose life and death 203
Of all the thoughts of God that are 168
Oh, deem not they are blessed alone 151
*Oh for the peace that floweth like a river 138
*Oh may I join the choir invisible 128
*Oh, yet we trust that somehow good 145
One adequate support 153
*O strong soul, by what shore 166
*O thicker, deeper, darker growing 162
Our beloved have departed 154

Quiet from God! how beautiful to keep 136

Rest, gentle traveller, on life's toilsome way 169

Servant of God, well done! 158
She waited for the summons, lengthening days . . . 208
Since thy Father's arm sustains thee 143
Sleep, tired one, sleep 176
Sometime, when all life's lessons have been learned . . 137
Straight and still the baby lies 183
Such beautiful, beautiful hands 206

Take them, O death, and bear away 111
The baby wept 189
The dead are like the stars by day 122
*The face which duly as the sun 108
The fragrance of the rose 115
The little feet that never trod 187
There is a Reaper whose name is Death 190
There is no death! The stars go down 146
There is no flock, however watched and tended . . . 202
There's not an hour but from some sparkling beach . . 122
They sat in peace in the sunshine 207
Those we love truly never die 142
Thou that art strong to comfort 143

	PAGE
To pass through life beloved as few are loved	159
To weary hearts, to mourning homes	139
Twilight falls, a tiny maiden	209
Until we meet again, that is the meaning	141
We know not what it is, dear	188
We must not doubt, or fear, or dread	147
*We need some charmer, for our hearts are sore	113
We watched her breathing through the night	200
We wreathed about our darling's head	197
What shall I do with all the days and hours	124
What may we take into the vast forever	127
What did we ask with all our love for him	176
Where the mountains slope to the westward	178
*Who is the angel that cometh? Life!	107
Why shouldst thou fear the beautiful angel Death?	125
*Wilt thou not ope thy heart to know?	130
*Within this lowly grave a conqueror lies	181
*Within the maddening maze of things	150

SUPPLEMENTARY LIST OF POEMS.

Reference is made to the following books: —

Putnam. Singers and Songs of the Liberal Faith. [Boston. Roberts.
Schaff & Gilman. Library of Religious Poetry. [N. Y. 1881.
Quiet Hours. 2 vols. [Boston. Roberts.
Bryant. Library of Poetry and Song. [N. Y. 1872
Chadwick, J. W. Poems. [Boston. Roberts.
Household Edition — Poems of Longfellow, Whittier, Lowell, Bryant, Alice and Phœbe Cary. [Boston, Houghton, Mifflin & Co.
Sunshine in the Soul. 2 vols. [Boston. Roberts.
Hymns of the Ages. 3 vols. [Boston. Houghton, Mifflin & Co.
Revised Hymn & Tune Book. [Boston. Amer. Unitarian Association.
Memory and Hope. [Boston. Ticknor & Fields. 1851
Sunday Book of Praise. Golden Treasury Series. [London. Macmillan.
Proctor, A. A. Poems. [Boston. 1880.
Verses, by "H. H." [Boston. Roberts.
Sursum Corda. [Boston. Roberts. 1877
Hosmer and Gannett. The Thought of God. [Boston. Roberts. 1885
Brooks, C. T. Memoir and Poems. [Boston. Roberts. 1885
Hemans, F. Poems. [Boston. 1833.
Lyra Americana. [N. Y. 1865.
Shadow of the Rock. [N. Y. Randolph.
The Changed Cross. "   "
Palace of the King. "   "
The Chamber of Peace. "   "
Uplands of God. "   "
Cheering Words. "   "

PART I. — LIFE AND DEATH.

FUNERAL HYMN . . . . *W. R. Alger.*
"The worlds that shine above us nightly."
                                      Putnam, 471

PRAYER AND THE DEAD . . . . *N. L. Frothingham.*
"They passed away from sight and hands."
              Putnam. 102. Quiet Hours, I., 149.

MORTAL AND IMMORTAL . . . . *R. C. Watterson.*
"I stand between the Future and the Past."
              Schaff & Gilman, 302. Putnam, 403

SUPPLEMENTARY POEMS.

SEALED ORDERS . . . . . . *J. W. Chadwick.*
"Our life is like a ship that sails some day."
                                    Poems, 136. Putnam, 518

HE AND SHE . . . . *Edwin Arnold.*
"She is dead," they said to him.
                                     Schaff & Gilman, 859

AFTER THE BURIAL . . . . *Lowell.*
"Yes, faith is a goodly anchor."
                                                  Poems, 353

THE CLOUD ON THE WAY . . . . . *Bryant.*
"See, before us in our journey."
                                                  Poems, 250

QUA CURSUM VENTUS . . . . . *A. H. Clough.*
"As ships becalmed at eve."
                                  Poems, 33. Quiet Hours, I., 69
(Friends separated by long absence, reunited.)

COMPENSATION . . . . *C. P. Cranch.*
"Tears wash away the atoms in the eye."
                                     Schaff & Gilman, 936

NOW AND AFTERWARDS . . . . *D. M. Mulock.*
"Two hands upon the breast."
                           Poems, 134. Bryant, Library, 177

THE VANISHERS . . . . *Whittier.*
"Sweetest of all childlike dreams."
                                                  Poems, 321

THE RIVER PATH . . . . *Whittier.*
"No birds's song floated down the bank."
                                                  Poems, 284

THE FUTURE LIFE . . . . *Bryant.*
"How shall I know thee in the sphere?"
                                                 Poems, 183

DEATH OF A CHRISTIAN . . . . . *J. D. Burns.*
"The apostle slept — a light shone in the prison."
                                    Shadow of the Rock, 20

COMING . . . . *Barbara Macandrew.*
"It may be in the evening."
(Death's uncertainty.)   Schaff & Gilman, 649

THE SOWER . . . . *R. W. Gilder.*
"A sower went forth to sow."
(The mission of pain.)   Schaff and Gilman, 826

HOW BEAUTIFUL TO BE ALIVE . . . *H. S. Sutton.*
"How beautiful it is to be alive!"
                                    Sunshine in the Soul, I., 94

HE LEADS HIS OWN . . . . *Hymns of the Ages.*
"How few who from their youthful day."
(The unexpected lot.)   Sunshine in the Soul, I., 89

SUPPLEMENTARY POEMS. 217

COME, YE DISCONSOLATE . . . . . *Moore.*
　　　　　　　　　　　　　Rev. H. & T. Book, 858
IN THE OTHER WORLD . . . . *H. B. Stowe.*
　"It lies around us like a cloud."
　　　　　　　　　　　　　Shadow of the Rock, 51
THE TWO WORLDS . . . . . *Dublin Univ. Mag.*
　"Two worlds there are. To one our eyes we strain."
　　　　　　　　　　　　　Shadow of the Rock, 133
NUNC SUSCIPE, TERRA . . . . . *Prudentius.*
　"Receive him, Earth, into thy harboring shrine."
　(At the grave.) 　　　　　　Book of Praise, 318
MORTALITY . . . . . *Mrs. Muloch-Craik.*
　"Ye dainty mosses, lichens gray."
　Hymns of the Ages, II., 240. Poems Old and New, 1881. 56
HYMN DURING THE PLAGUE . . . . *Prof. Wilson.*
　"The air of death breathes through our souls."
　　　　　　　　　　　　　Schaff & Gilman, 132
THE OTHER SIDE . . . . . . *Alice Cary.*
　"I dreamed I had a plot of ground."
　　　　　　　　　　　　　Poems, 135
THE VERDICT OF DEATH . . . . *Mrs. Charles.*
　"How doth Death speak of our Beloved?"
　　　Quiet Hours, II., 181. The Changed Cross, 150
FROM "IN MEMORIAM," XCII. . . . . *Tennyson.*
　"How pure at heart and sound in head."
　　　　　　　　　　　　　Quiet Hours, I., 150
HOMEWARD . . . . . . *Horatius Bonar.*
　"To my beloved ones my steps are moving."
　　　　　　　　　　　　　Palace of the King, 11
THERE . . . . *L. C. Moulton.*
　"Do any hearts ache there, beyond the peaceful river?"
　　　　　　　　　　　　　Palace of the King, 141
THE DEAD . . . . . . - . *H. Alford.*
　"The dead alone are great."
　　　　　　　　　　　　　Memory and Hope, 52
THE ANGEL AT THE TOMB . . . *S. F. Adams.*
　"The mourners came at break of day."
　　　　　　　　　　　　　Memory and Hope, 66
INCOMPLETENESS . . . . . *A. A. Proctor.*
　"Nothing resting in its own completeness."
　　　　　　　　　　　　　Poems, 53
THE RESURRECTION . . . . . . *Klopstock.*
　"Arise, yes, yes, arise, O thou my dust."
　　　　　　　　　　　　　Schaff & Gilman, 774

A LITTLE WAY . . . . *Anonymous.*
  "A little way — I know it is not far."
    Chamber of Peace, 20
THE PATH OF DEATH . . . . *Faber.*
  "How pleasant are thy paths, O death!"
    Rev. H. & T. Book, 693
SPINNING . . . . "*H. H.*"
  "Like a blind spinner in the sun."
    Quiet Hours, I., 59. Verses, 14

PART II. — RESIGNATION — TRUST.

HYMN OF TRUST . . . . . . *O. W. Holmes.*
  "O Love Divine, that stooped to share."
    Rev. H. & T. Book, 725
THE LAST LOOK . . . . . *O. W. Holmes.*
  "Behold! not him we knew."
    Putnam, 258
"STILL WILL WE TRUST THOUGH EARTH SEEMS DARK AND DREARY." . . . . *Burleigh.*
    Putnam, 316. Rev. H. & T. Book, 875
HERE AND THERE . . . . . . *Alice Cary.*
  "Here is the sorrow and sighing."
    Poems, 160
PALINGENESIS. (Last 3 stanzas.) . . . . *Longfellow.*
  "Into what land of harvests."
    Poems, 317
"STILL, STILL WITH THEE." . . . *H. B. Stowe.*
    Rev. H. & T. Book, 764
THE MYSTERY OF LIFE . . . . . *S. Greg.*
  "Slowly, slowly darkening."
    Sursum Corda, 265
THE DAY IS DONE . . . . . *Anonymous.*
  "The day is done: soft as a dream."
    Sursum Corda, 269
I WILL NOT FEAR . . . . . *Jane Roscoe.*
  "Thy will be done! I will not fear."
    Sursum Corda, 29
GOD KNOWETH . . . . . . *Anonymous.*
  "I know not what shall befall me."
    Sursum Corda, 123
THE PILLAR OF THE CLOUD . . . . *Newman.*
  "Lead, kindly Light!"
    Rev. H. & T. Book, 773

SUPPLEMENTARY POEMS. 219

"There is a land where beauty cannot fade."   *Uhland.*
                                     Hymns of the Ages, III, 57
INTIMATIONS . . . . *Alice Cary.*
    "There is a hovering about me."
                                        Poems, 138
OF ONE FLESH . . . . *Phœbe Cary.*
    "A man he was who loved the good."
(For an imperfect, erring life.)   Poems, 291
A LITTLE WHILE . . . . *Greville.*
    "A little while, and every fear."
                                Hymns of the Ages, II., 141
A LITTLE LONGER . . . . . . *Chr. Register.*
    "A little longer yet, a little longer."
                                Hymns of the Ages, II., 237
FAITH . . . . *W. H. Hurlbut.*
    "We will not weep, for God is standing by us."
                                  Rev. H. & T. Book, 734
UNITED BY DEATH . . . . . . *A. P. Stanley.*
    "Till Death us part."
(For a loving husband and wife.)   Uplands of God, 238
HE GIVETH SONGS IN THE NIGHT . . *John Page Hopps.*
    "We praise thee oft for hours of bliss."
                                Shadow of the Rock, 93
THE DEAD . . . . *Anonymous.*
    "Thou God of Love! beneath thy sheltering wings."
(At the grave.)   Hymns of the Ages, III., 281.   Book of Praise, 318
A DYING HYMN . . . . *Alice Cary.*
    "Earth with its dark and dreadful ills."
                                   Poems, 160
ALL SAINTS' DAY . . . . . *Mrs. Mulock-Craik.*
    "I shall find them again, I shall find them again."
                              Poems Old and New, 484
DEATH . . . . *Anonymous.*
    "There are who fear thy summons, Death!"
                              Hymns of the Ages, II, 241
GREEN PASTURES AND STILL WATERS . . *W. C. Gannett.*
    "Clear in memory's silent reaches."
                               The Thought of God, 37
A FIRST SORROW . . . . . . *A. A. Procter.*
    "Arise, this day shall shine."
                                   Poems, 49
FRIEND SORROW . . . . *A. A. Procter.*
    "Do not cheat thy heart and tell her."
                                    Poems, 8

FROM CHANGE TO THE UNCHANGING . . . *M. Farmingham.*
"Slow move the feet amid life's lengthening shadows."
(An old country home.) Uplands of God, 145
THE GATHERING PLACE . . . . *Christian Worker.*
"I know not where, beneath, above."
Uplands of God, 207
MY TRIUMPH . . . . *Whittier.*
"The autumn-time has come."
(What a hopeful man might wish said at his grave.) Poems, 351
LOOKING UNTO GOD . . . . . . *S. Longfellow.*
"I look to thee in every need."
Rev. H. & T. Book, 624
A GERMAN TRUST SONG . . . . . . *Lampertus.*
"Just as God leads me I would go."
Sursum Corda, 93
TRUST AND SUBMISSION . . . . *Andrews Norton.*
"My God, I thank thee."
Rev. H. & T. Book, 724
WHEN? . . . . *Susan Coolidge.*
"If I were told that I must die to-morrow."
Schaff & Gilman, 19. Sunshine in the Soul, II., 140
BLESSED ARE THEY THAT MOURN . . . . *Burleigh.*
"Oh deem not that earth's crowning bliss."
Putnam, 317
"FOREVER WITH THE LORD." . . . . *Montgomery.*
Rev. H. & T. Book, 700
THE MEETING PLACE . . . . . . *Anonymous.*
"Where the faded flowers shall freshen."
The Changed Cross, 9.
MY TIMES ARE IN THY HAND . . . . . *Waring.*
"Father, I know that all my life."
Rev. H. & T. Book, 502
THE LOVE OF GOD . . . . *Bryant.*
"All things that are on earth shall wholly pass away."
Poems, 149
FROM "IN MEMORIAM." . . . . . . *Tennyson.*
"Strong Son of God, immortal Love."
Quiet Hours, II., 193
GOD'S PRESENCE THE SOURCE OF ALL JOY . . *Dessler.*
"O Friend of souls, 'tis well with me."
Quiet Hours, II., 150
FLIGHT OF THE SPIRIT . . . . . *Mrs. Hemans.*
"Whither, oh, whither wilt thou wing thy way?"
Quiet Hours, II., 188

I Move into the Light . . . . . *Anonymous.*
"Out of the shadows that shroud the soul."
                          Palace of the King, 101

Lent, not Lost . . . . . . *Anonymous.*
"All is not lost that's passed beyond our keeping."
                          Palace of the King, 123

No More . . . . *Mrs. Gaskell.*
"No more, on earth no more."
                          Memory and Hope, 105

"While Thee I seek, protecting Power." *H. M. Williams.*
                          Rev. H. & T. Book, 238

"Nearer, my God, to Thee." . . . *S. F. Adams.*
                          Rev. H. & T. Book, 621

The Eternal Years . . . . . . *Faber.*
"How shalt thou bear the cross that now."
                          Unity Hymns and Chorals, 142

Death . . . . *Anonymous.*
"Out of the shadows of sadness."
                          Cheering Words, 190

Memory of H. N. S. . . . . . . *C. T. Brooks.*
"This is not all, — this fleeting world we see."
                          Poems, 147

Death of a Young Artist . . . . *C. T. Brooks.*
"The breath of morn and May."
                          Poems, 152

God Knoweth Best . . . . . . *F. H. Marr.*
"He took them from me, one by one."
(Trustful through many afflictions.)   Chamber of Peace, 114

"At Noontide came a Voice." . . . *Dora Greenwell.*
(A woman in prime of life.)   Sursum Corda, 273

PART III. — A GOOD LIFE.

In Memoriam. H. T. Tuckerman . . . *C. T. Brooks.*
"O friend, endeared to heart and mind."
                          Putnam, 362

In Memory of R. H. . . . . . *C. T. Brooks.*
"Lamb of God's fold!"
                          Putnam, 369

Charles Sumner . . . . *Longfellow.*
"Garlands upon his grave."
                          Poems, 358

THE SOUL'S PARTING . . . . . *Dora Greenwell.*
"She sat within life's Banquet Hall at noon."
                                      Sursum Corda, 275
DEATH AND SPRING . . . . . *J. W. Chadwick.*
"My noble friend is dead."
                                                Poems, 131
MEMORIAE POSITUM. (In part.) . . . . *Lowell.*
"Why make we moan?"
                                                Poems, 381
A KNIGHT-ERRANT . . . . . . *A. A. Procter.*
"Though he lived and died among us."
(Truth's Warrior.)   Poems, 18
FOLLEN. (In part.) . . . . . . *Whittier.*
"Oh, while life's solemn mystery glooms."
                                                Poems, 96
A LAMENT . . . . *Whittier.*
"The circle is broken, one seat is forsaken."
                                                Poems, 135
JOSEPH STURGE. (In part.) . . . . . *Whittier.*
"Thanks for the good man's beautiful example."
                                                Poems, 238
THE BLESSED LIFE . . . . . . *W. T. Mason.*
"O blessed life! the heart at rest."
                                       Rev. H. & T. Book, 233
IN MEMORIAM . . . . *Gerald Massey.*
"Why should we weep when 'tis so well with him?"
                                  A Tale of Eternity, etc., 135
DEATH OF A CHRISTIAN . . . . . *Mrs. Hemans.*
"Calm on the bosom of thy God."
                                           Rev. H. & T. Book, 715
"BROTHER, THOU ART GONE BEFORE US." . . *Milman.*
                                              Book of Praise, 322
A HAPPY DEATH . . . . *John Dryden.*
"As precious gums are not for lasting fire."
                     Quiet Hours, II., 163. Book of Praise, 169
SAFE . . . . *Alice Cary.*
"Ah, she was not an angel to adore."
                                                Poems, 137
"HOW BLEST THE RIGHTEOUS WHEN HE DIES." . *Barbauld.*
                                           Rev. H. & T. Book, 730
CHARACTER OF THE HAPPY WARRIOR . . *Wordsworth.*
"Who is the happy Warrior? Who is he?"
"THE GOOD,—THEY DROP AROUND US, ONE BY ONE."
                                                  Isaac Williams.
                                                 Quiet Hours, II., 166

SUPPLEMENTARY POEMS.   223

"Go to the grave in all thy glorious prime."
                                                Montgomery.
                              Rev. H. & T. Book, 756
Tribute to Bishop Heber   .   .   .   *Mrs. Hemans.*
           " If it be sad to speak of treasures gone."
(A wise and useful man.)   Poems, B. 1833, I., 187

PART IV. — SUFFERING — REST.

Decoration   .   .   .   .   .   .   *T. W. Higginson.*
           " 'Mid the flower-wreathed tombs I stand."
              Scribner's Monthly, June, 1874.   Putnam, 483
(For a woman heroic in suffering.)
Resting in Hope   .   .   .   .   .   .   *H. Bonar.*
           " Rest for the toiling hand."
                              Rev. H. & T. Book, 702
Bear out the Dead   .   .   .   .   .   .   *Haven.*
           " Ay, carry out your dead."
                              Schaff & Gilman, 886
Rest   .   .   .   .   .   .   *Euphemia Saxby.*
           " It was Thy will, my Father."
                              Quiet Hours, I., 144
The Gate of Heaven.   .   .   .   *Disciples Hymn Book.*
           " She stood outside the gate of Heaven."
(For an ill life.)   Quiet Hours, I., 162
"Ah, well! she had her will."
                              Sursum Corda, 279
(For one who suffered secretly, and was misunderstood.)
On his Blindness   .   .   .   .   .   .   *Milton.*
(For one blind.)
"Thou Knowest, Lord, the weariness and sorrow."
                                            Jane Borthwick.
                              Sursum Corda, 30
From "Miriam."   .   .   .   .   .   .   *Whittier.*
           " Wherever through the ages rise the altars of self-sacrifice."
                              Poems, 342
"Going Home."   .   .   .   .   .   *Anonymous.*
           "'Heimgang!' So the German people."
(For a German family.)   Uplands of God, 53
The Sweet Surprise. (In part.)   .   .   .   *Anonymous.*
           " Down to the borders of the silent land."
(For one who lingered.)   Uplands of God, 69

THE E'EN BRINGS A' HAME . . . . . *Anonymous.*
   "Upon the hills the wind is sharp and cold."
               Shadow of the Rock, 68

GONE HOME . . . . *Anonymous.*
   "Gone home! She lingers here no longer."
               The Changed Cross, 211

CALLED ASIDE . . . . *Anonymous.*
   "Called aside, — from the glad working of thy busy life."
               Palace of the King, 94.

GOOD-NIGHT . . . . *Anonymous.*
   "If I could only lay me down to rest."
               Palace of the King, 130

OUR CALVARY . . . . *F. P. Cobbe.*
   "God draws a cloud over each gleaming morn."
               Unity Hymns and Chorals, 148

THE CHAMBER OF PEACE . . . . . *Anonymous.*
   "After the burden and heat of the day."
(The serenity of the dead.)   The Chamber of Peace, 5

CHARLOTTE CUSHMAN . . . . . . *C. T. Brooks.*
   "For wast not thou, too, going forth alone."
               Poems, 141

PART V. — CHILDHOOD — YOUTH.

THE DEATH OF CHILDREN . . . . *J. Q. Adams.*
   "Sure to the mansions of the blest."
               Putnam 12

"SHE IS NOT DEAD, BUT SLEEPETH." . . . . *Furness.*
               Putnam, 165

TO J. S. . . . . *W. W. Story.*
               Poems, 1856, 228

THE CHILD'S PICTURE . . . . . *F. E. Abbot.*
   "Little face, so sweet, so fair."
               Quiet Hours, I., 155

"CHILDISH FEET ARE STRAYING HOMEWARD."
               Bartholomew, "The Comforter."

WHERE? . . . . *J. W. Chadwick.*
   "That is her body lying there."
               Poems, 145

KINSMAN . . . . *Whittier.*
   "Where ceaseless Spring her garland twines."
(One dying away from home.)   Poems, 392

SUPPLEMENTARY POEMS.

Lines to the Memory of "Annie." . . *H. B. Stowe.*
 "In the fair gardens of celestial peace."
  Bryant's Library, 176

Suffer little Children . . . . . *Elim.*
 "They are going — only going."
  Rev. H. & T. Book, 751

The Discoverer . . . . . . *Stedman.*
 "I have a little kinsman."
  Schaff & Gilman, 879

Fire . . . . *John Keble.*
 "Sweet maiden, for so calm a life."
 (An elder sister.) Book of Praise, 204

A Dead Baby . . . . . . *Mrs. Mulock-Craik.*
 "Little soul, for such brief space that entered."
  Poems, Old and New, 123

Dying, and yet Living . . . . . *Theo. Tilton.*
 "She died — yet is not dead."
  Lyra Americana, 213

Early Lost, Early Saved . . . *Geo. W. Bethune.*
 "Within her downy cradle there lay a little child."
  Lyra Americana, 222

She Came and Went . . . . . *Lowell.*
 "As a twig trembles when a bird."
  Poems, 90

My Lambs . . . . *Anonymous.*
 "I loved them so."
  The Changed Cross, 78

At a Death Bed . . . . . . *C. H. Dall.*
 "Dear eyes, that never looked reproach."
  Putnam, 533

To the Memory of William Power Watts . *A. A. Watts.*
 "A cloud is on my heart and brow."
  Memory and Hope, 33

Mabel . . . . *A. R. W.*
 "Like broken thoughts in dreams."
  Memory and Hope, 102

Two . . . . *Chamber's Journal.*
 "Two buds plucked from the tree."
 (For twin children.) Shadow of the Rock, 142

Dirge for a Young Girl . . . . *J. T. Fields.*
 "Underneath the sod low lying."
  Bryant's Library, 190

HERMAN . . . . *J. F. Clarke.*
   "Where is my boy?"
        Memory and Hope, 58

"WHEN THE BABY DIED" . . . . . *H. H.*
   Schaff & Gilman, 876. Verses, 100

"CHILD WITH THE SNOWY CHEEK." . . *W. H. Savage.*
   Savage's Minister's Handbook, 100

THRENODIA . . . . *Lowell.*
   "Gone, gone from us."
           Poems, 1

PART VI. — OLD AGE.

THE FINISHED LIFE . . . . . . *M. J. Savage.*
   "There's a beauty of the Spring-time."
     Savage's Minister's Handbook.

IN MEMORY . . . . *Anonymous.*
   "Close, kind hands, the aged eyes."
     Songs of Two Worlds, 131

ONLY WAITING . . . . *Anonymous.*
   "Only waiting till the shadows."
     Rev. H. & T. Book, 746

"SERVANT OF GOD, WELL DONE!" . . *Montgomery.*
     Rev. H. & T. Book, 711

RIPE WHEAT . . . . *Anonymous.*
   "We bent to-day o'er a coffined form."
      Cheering Words, 71

GRACE OF GOD . . . . *Eliza Scudder.*
   "Thou Grace Divine, encircling all."
     Rev. H. & T. Book, 304

O THOU before whose sight all generations of men pass over to their rest, to thee alone can we turn in this hour. Amid all life's changes thou art the same forever, and thy years shall have no end. Thou art the source of all life. Thou art the Power above all powers and Lord of Death. To thee we come, who dost clothe the grass of the field, and mark the falling sparrow. To thy unfailing compassion we look, thou who dost note thy children's pain and grief. We bring these empty hearts, this loneliness, this sorrow, and lay them at thy feet. Thou knowest it all, our Father, and because thou knowest, canst help us. Comfort us with thy love, greater than a mother's love for her child! Send thy pity to lighten the darkness; send thy patience that we may bear this trial bravely. Touch these wounds with thy hand of healing, and help us to be still.

Almighty Father, give us of thy strength that we may take up our lives more bravely for the sake of this dear one who has now done with earth. May we learn to be faithful in duty, thoughtful, tender of others, loyal to the service of holiness and truth, because of those who can work no longer here on earth. May we think not of our loss, our suffering, but of their release, of the peace that rests upon this mortal body, and the freedom wherein the soul has now found a higher joy.

Grant, we pray thee, the faith that these ties of affection — the holiest thing thou givest us to know — can never perish. Wheresoever this dear friend may go, he can not be forgetful of us, and henceforth we are no more strangers to the life beyond since these have entered to make it home.

Now, Almighty Creator, into thy hands we commend

the spirit thou didst give. We thank thee for the memory of his life. No longer can we care for him; but thou wilt care for him better than our love could do. By pastures green and by quiet waters, into new realms of purity and love and truth, into new and higher labors in thy service thou wilt lead him. Cherish and keep him, we pray thee, and through ways unknown to us bring him at last nearer to thy Presence, O God of the Living and the Dead!

And when we, too, are called to bid farewell to this world of love and beauty, of joy and sorrow, grant that we may follow after him. Grant that our love may grow stronger in these years of absence. Bring us, if it be thy purpose with us, bring us together again where we may know each other better. May we trust the highest instincts of this human heart, telling us that the love which conquers death is forever immortal. We ask in the memory of Jesus, our Elder Brother. In memory of his tender heart, his courage and purity, we would be lifted up into his peace, and learn with him to pray: Thy will, not ours, O God! Thou didst give, and thou hast taken away. Blessed be the name of the Lord!

C. J. S.

O Thou who art the Beginning and the End of all lives, in whom the living live and the dead sleep, grant that we in the presence of death may feel that our true life is in thee. Thou who hast made us as we are made, to love life, and to grieve and suffer in the presence of death, be near to us when we call upon thy name, feeling in that presence we have no help save in thee alone. It is our comfort and consolation in turning our hearts to thee, when they are made heavy by sorrow, that thou art greater than our hearts and knowest all things. When our grief is too great to be uttered, and our need is more and deeper than we know or can express, thou knowest it altogether. Thy hand, Father Almighty, has fashioned the ties that bind us one to another in love and friendship, and when those ties are broken by death, that which we have to suffer is known to thee alone. We desire to feel, though we cannot know that thy will in trouble and affliction is not to punish us but to bless us; that alike in all we are born to suffer in our affections, and in all the happiness and enjoyment we derive from them, the pity and goodness of the Highest are manifested and expressed. We desire in our darkest hours to trust thee, and against doubts and fears that test us and perplex us, to cling to the belief that all is for the best, not meant to crush us or to extinguish our hopes and desires for those we love and for ourselves, but to work out for them and for us good beyond our belief and hope.

When our faith is weak, and heart and flesh faint and fail, good Lord, have mercy upon us; in thy mercy remember us; in thy pity visit us, that in the thought of thy pity we may be saved from despair of ourselves. Thou knowest how hard it is for us to assure ourselves, when those we love better than life are taken from us, that we are not forgotten or disowned by Him that made us, that our loss is not all loss, and our suffering and anguish not all vain and fruitless. Our affections cling to that which is earthly and familiar to us, so that it is hard for us to think and feel that our beloved dead, whose faces we shall no more behold, are still with thee, and that in thy presence and dominion death hath no more dominion over them.

Like as a father pitieth his children, so the Lord pitieth them that fear him. Even as we are moved by pity for the weak, and downcast, and sorrowful, so our hearts assure us it must be that He who is the highest of all must be the best of all, pitiful and compassionate beyond our belief and hope, to all that lives and breathes.

Grant, our Father, that we may in all trouble that is darkest and deepest, find in this revelation of thyself within us, thy consolation ministered to us, and thy light lightening our darkness.

Help of all the sorrowful, Comforter of all that mourn, we remember in thy presence, those whose share in the sorrow we feel this day is heaviest and sorest. Comfort them by the sympathy of friends, and much more by thy grace. Consecrate this sorrow for all of us who have part in it, and grant that even what is darkest and most mysterious in it, may not be without profit in showing us and opening for us the path of life.

We remember in thy presence, now and here, all the children of sorrow. above all those whose sorrow like ours this day, is for the dead, concerning whom their souls refuse to be comforted. In the darkness and mystery in which their lives are shrouded, may light arise for them, and shine upon them from the sympathy of their kind, much more from thee the First and the Last, thou whose tender mercies are over all thy works, who knoweth our frame, who remembereth that we are dust.

JOHN SERVICE.

www.ingramcontent.com/pod-product-compliance
Lightning Source LLC
Chambersburg PA
CBHW021807230426
43669CB00008B/661